TAO OF OLD SCHOOL BOXING

THE DEFINITIVE GUIDE TO KNOCKOUT POWER

WRITTEN BY JAMES CARSS
WITH ILLUSTRATIONS BY RICHARD GORE

Mojo Risin'
Publishing Ltd

Published in 2021 by Mojo Risin' Publishing Ltd
www.mojorisinpublishing.com

British Library Cataloguing in Publication Data:
A catalogue record for this book is available from
the British Library

ISBN-13:
978-1-9163867-8-5

Cover design
David Stanyer

Layout
Neil Jackson, Media Arts
www.media-arts.co.uk

Printed & bound by PrintGuy
Proudly published Up North

To every fighter who has ever felt the rush of fear, adrenaline and excitement of stepping into the ring to face another fighter, risking life, humiliation and defeat.

"I was a miner and I was a cowboy but mostly I was a hobo.
I fought wherever I could, in school halls, outside saloons, any place they were putting up a purse. I once walked thirty miles across the desert to a town called Goldfield in Nevada so I could fight for twenty dollars.
I got beat a lot. I improved. But I remember the beatings I took.
Once I got beat so bad they had to take me out of the ring in a wheelbarrow.
Later some said I was a killer in the ring. They got that wrong.
I killed nobody. But I took out other guys quick. That much is true. I got more one round knockouts than anybody, sixty knockouts in the first round.
I beat a good Heavyweight in New Orleans once in fourteen seconds.
I knocked out Fred Fulton, six-foot-four, 250 pounds, in nineteen seconds.
How come? Not because I was a killer. Other way round.
I was always afraid that I'd be the one who was killed.
Get 'em quick and you live to fight another day."

- Jack Dempsey

Contents

Part One: Background

Contents

Part Two: Skill Acquisition

Part Three: Punching Mechanics

Part Four: Old School Training

Foreword By Glenn McCrory

When my good pal Steve Wraith told me about a book he was publishing about old school boxing I was intrigued to say the least. As the former IBF Cruiserweight world champion and a man who has been in there with the likes of Lennox Lewis, I like to think I know a thing or two about throwing a punch. Lets' not forget I was the sparring partner to the meanest man on the planet who features prominently in this book. Mr. Tyson or Mike as I called him was absolutely lethal and knocked out a string of men who couldn't hack the pace before they flew me over to Atlantic City. I took it in my stride and never let the man get close enough to do any real damage, it was tough don't get me wrong, but we sparred hundreds of rounds and I never quit once.

I'm happy to agree with Steve that the 'The Tao of Old School Boxing' is a long overdue book that brings boxing back to its roots and examines the core of the art. Fellow Geordie James Carss has done a brilliant job in his research and knowledge.

James' painstaking examination of the skills of great boxers (where was I?) will be relevant to fight fans and aspiring boxers alike. Certainly, I found it a very enjoyable read. in my own case, as a young lad growing up in County Durham, I'd have got my teeth stuck right into this.

'The Tao of Old School Boxing' is a great milestone and terrific read, as Tyneside's only former World Champion Boxer I put my stamp of approval on this and hope it can inspire a local young lad or lass to take up the sport and do something great.

Glenn McCrory
IBF World Cruiseweight Champion
August 2021

Introduction: Old School Is The Best School

Boxing is a fighting art as old as mankind. From the ancient Greek Olympics to English bare knuckle prize fighting, where savage and bloody contests often ended in death. Fighters not only participated for money to be able to eat and live, but they risked death and often fought for their lives. Make no mistake, in the noble art of boxing the object was to destroy the opponent conclusively, there was no point scoring, or stick and move contest, there was but one winner and he was the last one standing with a pulse.

A golden age for boxing, which included a dramatic transformation and evolution of form, occurred 1900-1940. These were troubled times with two horrific World Wars and boxing became a symbol of both national pride and strength. The art became more sophisticated and developed from brutality into the 'sweet science'. During this period boxing transitioned from bare knuckle to gloves, but the essence remained the same; win at all costs.

After this 'golden period' we saw a gradual decline in the level of boxers from a raw power perspective. That is of course not to say great punchers and knock out artists did not come along after that time; several great ones did. We shall also examine some of those individuals, they went against the grain in a combat art that was quickly changing into a sport. These fighters went against the grain, they were not interested in running and employing defensive tactics to win a fight, nor were they satisfied with winning on points, these men had refined brute force and savagery into a systematic method of destroying another. The intention of this book is to both an attempt to preserve that lost art and provide the reader with a light walk through boxing history. This study is divided into two main sections: In part one we look at developing the basic tools of boxing; stances, punches and footwork. If you are interested in boxing's defensive skills such as, blocking, dodging, slipping and ducking and so on – you will need to select another book. We are primarily concerned with exploring the skill and power needed to knock another man out. We continue the study examining history, styles, and great fighters who helped shape and advance this evolution of the sweet science. In part 2 we focus on developing 'real' skill from grasping the basics to becoming a knockout artist of the highest order.

It is my hope that the reader will gain knowledge and insight from these fighting secrets that have become lost in the sands of time. I hope it has something for everyone from armchair boxing fans, historians, boxers, fighters and martial artists.

James Carss
August 2021

Chapter One: A Brief Walk Through Boxing History

The history of boxing goes back to Grecian times and we know the Olympic Games held at Olympia Greece, which included boxing, date back to 776 years B.C.

The early days of English prize fighting are best shown in the following timeline of many (but not all) notable pugilistic events:

1719 James Figg declared to be the first champion of England. During and after his reign he taught the arts of broadsword, cudgel and fist in the Adam and Eve pub on what is now Tottenham Court Road.

1734 The 'father' of Boxing was said to be Jack Broughton who established the 'Broughton rules' of the ring, which became accepted until 1838. Broughton had killed one of his opponents George Stevenson with a punch to the heart and was so affected that he used his influence to regulate boxing and make it safer.

1792 Dan Mendoza was the supreme champion and one of the first to develop scientific techniques of boxing and teach in gymnasiums. He was defeated by John Jackson who gave boxing lessons to notable members of society such as Lord Byron. Boxing became very fashionable during this time.

1800 Jim Belcher becomes undisputed champ after defeating Andrew Gamble of Ireland. He became blind in 1803 after an unfortunate racquet accident and was forced to retire at the age of 22. Though he came out of retirement and fought several more times, sadly he died at the age of 30 after losing his health and wealth.

1805 John Gulley fights the champion Henry Pearce, Gulley is knocked out in the 64th round but later goes on to be a boxing champion and successful businessman and a member of parliament.

1810 Tom Cribb beats American champion Tom Molineaux and repeats the same result in a rematch in 1811.

1823 Tom Spring defeats Jack Langan in front of a crowd of 30,000 in a fight lasting 149 minutes.

1833 James Burke becomes champion by beating and killing Simon Byrne. Burke becomes the first British boxer to fight in America, and was beating American champion Sam O'Rourke until an angry mob stormed the ring and tried to lynch Burke as all hell broke loose.

1835 Bendigo aka William Thompson beats Ben Caunt after 22 rounds when

Caunt is disqualified for hitting Bendigo whilst he was resting in his corner between rounds.

1860 The last great prizefight. Tom Sayers of Brighton fights John Heenan of New York. the fight is stopped after 41 rounds (2 hours and 6 minutes) with both men in terrible condition.

1867 The Marquess of Queensberry introduced his rules and the future of boxing forever changed. Gloves were introduced, 3-minute rounds with 1-minute rest periods that were capped and decided on points if no knockout prevailed. Bare knuckle prize fighting still existed alongside the new boxing but was in decline as boxing's popularity gained momentum.

1892 James 'Gentleman Jim' Corbett, a boxer of the new era who practiced scientific technique and conditioning, defeated prize fighter John L Sullivan the last great prize fighter who was as tough as they ever came. It was a passing of the torch.

Like many sports over the course of time boxing has changed significantly in terms of style, technique and method. In other sports, developments in science and technology have contributed greatly to this change. For example, in tennis the evolution of the racket from a wooden to a carbon fiber ergonomically developed tool transformed and changed the game. In athletics, analysis of biomechanical imagery has contributed to changing and perfecting movements in both running and jumping. Interestingly, in boxing neither of these factors have played much part. Technology plays almost no factor in the sport bedside perhaps gloves and protective equipment, which are more for self-preservation than performance enhancement. The study of Biomechanics has not changed the techniques - with no agreed perfect punch mechanics. If anything it could be argued that technique has degraded over the years with the loss of knowledgeable expert trainers.

A key reason for the changes to boxing are the impact of a few notable fighters who were pioneers of certain methods and styles that changed the development of boxing forever. This gets quite complex to analyse as styles cross over periods in development, but now and again a truly unique talent appeared that contributed to a change in ideas.

With the onset of gloves in 1867 to around 1920 the major style of boxing was the British style that carried over from the bareknuckle days. Gloves were still new in this period. Fighters were very tough and fought over 25 rounds and more, power and fitness were critical. Style generally comprised:

- Erect posture, short stance and knees relatively straight.
- Guard held low, at waist level with arms extended.

- Weight distribution in favour of rear leg.
- Combinations of 2 to 4 punches employed but infrequently.
- "One- two" made up the high percentage of attacks.
- Mix of body and head punches.
- Punches generally long and straight.
- In-fighting defense well honed.

In 1908, Jack Johnson defeated Tommy Burn to become world heavy-weight champion. He was rather unique with incredible defensive skills and countering ability. However, with his exception it was the lighter class fighters that displayed higher skills than their heavier counterparts. They could fight at short and mid-range and displayed balance, pivoting, superior body positioning, increased head movement and correct delivery of punches with excellent body mechanics.

By the 1920s the skills of the lighter fighters began to emerge in all divisions and the level of boxing was very different, new skills included:

- Lateral footwork
- Complex and longer punching combinations
- Slipping and countering
- Feinting
- Counterpunching
- Crouching stances and higher guards

Skill and technique was becoming as important as power, toughness and conditioning. The downside of this change was the loss of infighting exper-tise and short and middle range punching, as this became less utilized. There was also the loss of evasion skills used with infighting.

In 1921, Jack Dempsey of America defeated Georges Carpentier of France in 4 rounds in the first 1-million-dollar gate. Dempsey was an exponent of the American style that comprised of fighting from a deep crouch, bobbing and weaving and throwing combinations of punches from every angle imagin-able.

Joe Louis is widely regarded by many as the most technically perfect heavyweight champion that ever lived, he reigned supreme from 1937-1949. From the mid 1950's-1960's professional clubs began to close and amateur boxing became more popular. Fighters frequently boxed 100+ fights as an ama-teur and turned professional at a later age. A significant change occurred in box-ing at this time and actually saw certain technical skills become less frequent as fighters adopted the amateur style, this included the loss of:

- Infighting
- Body snatching

• Short and middle range punching

Fighters were becoming more used to headhunting and being more predictable - taking turns to score with headshot combinations.

The continuation of amateur boxing techniques has resulted in amateur-focussed, less experienced coaches and trainers. This has continued to the modern day and we've gradually seen the erosion of real skill in boxing. There are still great fighters around today but they are a minority and far less common than in days gone by.

John L. Sullivan

Chapter Two: Boxing Styles

It would seem more often than not that over the course of time all great fighters come unstuck at some point (with a few minor exceptions). It is often part of the learning process and, indeed, coming back from and learning from defeat is what makes a great champion. It is often also true that the person to first defeat a champion often goes nowhere or fades into oblivion thereafter. Can you name all the fighters who defeated Muhammad Ali? Who did Buster Douglas beat after Mike Tyson, how will Andy Ruiz's career go after beating Anthony Joshua?

Boxing is a complex art. Take the 100-metre sprint in an Olympic final; it is hard to argue against the fact that the fastest and strongest sprinter will win on the day. In boxing It's not always the better man, it's the strategy behind the brains, the boxing IQ. More often this is contained within an individual style of a fighter that may be the perfect match to defeat one fighter, or be a hand in a lions cage to another.

Style in boxing comprises:

* Personality – direct, passive, aggressive.
* Individual attributes – speed, power, fitness, durability
* Body type – tall, short, thick, thin.

We can then categorise those styles to 4 distinct types:

* The Pure Boxer
* The Infighter
* The Slugger
* The Boxer Puncher

It is possible for some boxers to be a hybrid of two or more styles and also even change their style over time to meet another category.

The pure boxer is a long-range boxing style characteristic of 'outfighting' long range defensive techniques utilising clever footwork and a quick jab. Gene Tunney and Muhammed Ali are classic examples from the past. Today Tyson Fury would meet these criteria. These fighters don't generally knock out opponents but win on points, lack of power is compensated for by timing, speed and IQ.

The infighter is the most aggressive. It is a style that comprises non-stop pressure punching, closing the gap – all good infighters have fast feet, head movement, ability to take punishment and punching power. Tyson, Dempsey and Rocky Marciano are great examples of this style.

The slugger has the hardest punch and ability to KO their opponent but lacks finesse, footwork and can be predictable, often waiting and seeking the one big shot. If that shot connects though it can be a sleeping tablet for anyone. George Foreman, Sonny Liston and Rocky Graziano were all sluggers.

Finally, Boxer- Punchers. A harder style to immediately recognise, they have hand speed, counter punching ability, are better at defence than a slugger but not to the level of a pure boxer. They are still a dangerous puncher but not as high pressure as an infighter. Joe Louis, Sugar Ray Leonard and Tommy Hearns all fit this category.

It gets interesting when two of the same styles meet: two pure boxer fighters can be long winded and strategic like a game of chess, two sluggers more like a time bomb waiting to go off at any moment.

When two opposing styles meet it gets really interesting. If skill levels and experience are similar then generally pure boxers beat sluggers, sluggers beat infighters. Boxer-punchers often do well against infighters but struggle with sluggers. Of course, an outstanding boxer can adopt one style and beat anyone but in an even match up a specific style is good to fight one style but bad against another.

Chapter Three: The Gatti Vs Ward Saga

In 2002 two fighters came together in a fight that was not for any championship belt but a fight that would go down in history as one of the most aggressive and relentless encounters ever. It produced arguably one of the most brutal, competitive and entertaining rounds in boxing history. Ultimately this encounter would lead to a trilogy of fights with 30 rounds of non-stop savagery. These three fights were a throwback to an age long gone when fighters had the hunger to survive and kill when necessary, when individuals fought in order to live. Such blood and guts is rarely seen in the modern era. The great Jack Dempsey once said:

"When I was a young fellow, I was knocked down plenty. I wanted to stay down, but I couldn't. I had to collect the two dollars for winning or go hungry. I had to get up. I was one of those hungry fighters. You could have hit me on the chin with a sledgehammer for five dollars. When you haven't eaten for two days you'll understand."

The first fight between Gatti and Ward was voted Ring Magazine fight of the year and it also announced that the winner would be named 'boxing's ultimate blood and guts warrior'. Make no mistake these two men were among the toughest of their own era. Ward a vicious body puncher with a unrelentless style and ability to take a punch. Gatti was perhaps the better overall fighter and a knockout artist with little defence or inclination to ever take the back foot. His style was to go to war and go all out on the attack. Putting these two gladiators together in the ring created an epic match of styles.

The brawling didn't commence until round three when Ward started to unleash menacing body hooks slowing down Gatti who had previously dominated with superior distance and timing. In round 4 Gatti had a point deducted for a low blow, which he apologised for at the end of the round. This demonstrated the respect and sportsmanship between the two fighters, again a flashback to the past when boxers were gentlemen and had manners and values along with brawn.

In round five 88 of the 98 punches thrown were clean power shots, both men's chins were tested to the extreme. The fight swung both ways between the sixth and the eight with Gatti narrowly ahead on points as they came out for the now historic and epic 9th round, which has been labelled as round of the century.

Ward landed 60 power punches compared to Gatti's 42. The left body hooks of Ward were taking their toll on Gatti seeing him dropped to his knee and almost counted out but up at the ninth count. The round was toe to toe with both fighters dishing out and absorbing incredible amounts of punishment. It was a war like something out of a Rocky movie with Ward gaining the edge by the end. In the tenth round the action continued but both fighters were at the absolute point of exhaustion, neither raising the hand of victory when the final bell rang.

Ultimately, although Ward won this first encounter on points and Gatti took the next two fights, the outcomes seem less important than the memory of these three fights producing epic battles like the bare knuckle brawls of the past.

Gatti (left) V Ward

Chapter Four: Skill In Boxing

Great fighters are masters of their art. To be slick, skilful and a true exponent of the sweet science three things are required:

1. Boxing IQ. To be able to think clearly in a split second and change and adapt strategy as required.

2. Timing and distance. To read a punch, both from yourself and your opponent, to understand that a microsecond or an inch can mean the difference between success and failure.

3. Power. Not raw muscular power or 'strength' but the ability to both synchronize and co-ordinate the joints and tissue of the body into a chain reaction that releases energy like a whip.

Boxing brains or IQ gives a fighter the uncanny ability to think three or four steps ahead, to throw those first shots in round 1 and have the opponent completely mapped out and unmasked. This skill will enable the fighter to punish mistakes and set traps for the opponent. They can make their opponent do things they don't want to do, make them move into space where they want them and make them open up where they want to attack.

Timing and distance are critical to not waste energy and resources. Pinpoint precision and accuracy will always lead to damage and potential KO. This also applies to defence, not just to evade a blow by being out of range but to just miss and be in a perfect position to counter. Running from a fight is not boxing, to evade and being out of range is not skill but cowardliness. Whilst footwork is critical it is not the only component in timing and distance, being in perpetual motion with small slipping, bobbing and weaving can all achieve this.

Power - some say it is born, others say it can be nurtured. We will examine this later but for now we mean by definition the perfect knockout punch. Some fighters seem to just have danger in their fists, they are heavy savage hitters that make every punch count. The ability to hit through a guard, wear down an opponent and cause unrelenting punishment only comes through power and heavy hitting. Great fighters have bombs in both hands and can release them from every known angle with the same damaging consequences for the opponent.

Chapter Five: Out With The New, In With The Old

Are boxers better and more powerful now than 50 years ago? If we look at the knockout percentage in fighter's records it would indicate that fighters today generally have higher percentage with the exception of a few boxers who adopt a hit and run defensive style (Floyd Mayweather and Tyson Fury spring to mind). The higher percentage is actually misleading for several reasons, firstly, the quality of opposition means everything.

Back in the day it was very rare for fighters to avoid each other, people contested to be the undisputed champ. Nowadays, we have multiple organisations, governing bodies and belts – meaning several 'world' champions at each weight. Those champions have often had shortened amateur careers and then a series of low-class opposition fights to build a 'respectable' record. This did not happen in the past. Fighters were tough and game and frequently fought across multiple weight categories.

Consider the following men of the past:

- Bob Fitzsimmons a middleweight had 47 knockouts in his 54 wins, he knocked out heavyweight contenders Gus Ruhlin in six, Peter Maher in one, and Tom Sharkey, in two rounds.
- Stanley Ketchel scored 50 knockouts in his 54 wins, 19 were in three rounds or less.
- Sam Langford had more knockouts than Mike Tyson and George Foreman combined. A total of 138 career knockouts.
- Joe Gans scored 70 knockouts that were in 10 rounds or less, and 27 knockouts that were in three rounds or less.

Today in a world of pay per view a lot of boxing is geared to commercialisation, many boxers are undefeated but have never really been tested; has-beens, nobody's and stool pigeons do not make the fighter great. Another factor is the calibre of coaches and trainers, I would go as far on this topic to say boxing is becoming a lost art that was of higher calibre in the past. A good example would be Great Britain's Anthony Joshua, former Olympic heavyweight gold champion who ran for an unbeaten record (with more than a 90% KO ratio) to his 23rd fight. He then fought an unknown Mexican named Andy Ruiz who was a short notice, stand in opponent. Except for an aging Klitschko Joshua had beaten nobody of real note, he was a tremendous athlete and had unbelievable conditioning along with a decent punch and disciplined guard. However, there was something very robotic about his style, very little head movement and fluidity, he appeared very static. Ruiz upset the bookies big time with KO of Joshua in round 7. It did not surprise those in the know, Ruiz fought in the old way from a deep crouch with lateral movement and a great deal of head movement, punching from all angles. Joshua could not cope. Team GB had trained

Joshua with CrossFit and sport science, Ruiz had been trained in old school Mexican boxing by his family.

The sad truth about boxing is that it is becoming a lost art. Size and conditioning have taken over as the primary method that fighters are made and trained with. The actual level of skill and ability has diminished. It's not the volume or type of training fighters do – skipping, bag work, pad work, shadow boxing, repetition etc. It is the knowledge behind the training that develops the skill and the techniques. The old famous trainers were veterans of the game, ex fighters with hundreds of fights themselves who could teach a craft. Nowadays we have strength and conditioning experts, sport psychologists and massage therapists, but does anyone actually understand boxing? The talent is there but the masters with the ability to craft and hone that talent are becoming more and more rare.

Here is a final fact that may surprise the reader. The lightweight championship of the world in 1910 went on for 42 rounds, the fighters averaged 85 punches a round each. Compare that to a modern-day classic, Gatti vs Ward 3, in 2003. Gatti averaged 71 punches a round. for 10 rounds and that was regarded by many pundits as a modern-day boxing battle royale.

The fighters of the past did not just hit harder, but they went at it at a harder pace than today and over many more rounds. Old school boxing champions were better than what we see today. This book attempts to unlock and rediscovers those skills and secrets of an age long gone.

Chapter Six: The Ring Top 100 Greatest Punchers

In 2003, Ring Magazine published a list of the 100 greatest punchers of all time in boxing. The magazines writers voted on inclusions and used a multitude of criteria including knockout win percentage of fights, number of knockouts, quality of opposition and also when they came unstuck. As we have already seen there is a multitude of factors needed to make an assessment of a great knockout artist.

This list has every fighter included but of course the order could be argued all day long.

1. Joe Louis
2. Sam Langford
3. Jimmy Wilde
4. Archie Moore
5. Sandy Saddler
6. Stanley Ketchel
7. Jack Dempsey
8. Bob Fitzsimmons
9. George Foreman
10. Earnie Shavers
11. Sugar Ray Robinson
12. Ruben Olivares
13. Wilfredo Gomez
14. Rocky Marciano
15. Sonny Liston
16. Mike Tyson
17. Bob Foster
18. Thomas Hearns
19. Khaosai Galaxy
20. Alexis Arguello
21. Carlos Zarate
22. Max Baer
23. Rocky Graziano
24. Matthew Saad Muhammad
25. Julian Jackson
26. Danny Lopez
27. Gerald McClellan
28. Roberto Duran
29. Rodrigo Valdez
30. Felix Trinidad
31. Pipino Cuevas
32. James J. Jeffries
33. Lennox Lewis
34. Bennie Briscoe
35. Marvin Hagler
36. Edwin Rosario
37. Tommy Ryan
38. John Mugabi
39. Joe Frazier
40. Carlos Monzon
41. Tony Zale
42. Michael Spinks
43. Joe Gans
44. Elmer Ray
45. George Godfrey
46. Naseem Hamed
47. Alfonso Zamora
48. David Tua
49. Cleveland Williams
50. Julio Cesar Chavez
51. Tiger Jack Fox
52. Joe Walcott
53. Gerry Cooney
54. Al (Bummy) Davis
55. Max Schmeling
56. Florentino Fernandez
57. Henry Armstrong
58. Bob Satterfield
59. Al Hostak
60. Jesus Pimentel
61. Cyclone Hart
62. Lew Jenkins
63. Harry Wills
64. Tom Sharkey

65. Terry McGovern
66. Jersey Joe Walcott
67. Kostya Tszyu
68. Leotis Martin
69. Buddy Baer
70. Donovan (Razor) Ruddock
71. Jose Luis Ramirez
72. Tommy Gomez
73. Jose Napoles
74. Kid McCoy
75. Antonio Esparragoza
76. Ricardo Moreno
77. Evander Holyfield
78. Ike Williams
79. Luis Angel Firpo
80. Ricardo Lopez
81. Humberto Gonzalez
82. Bobby Chacon
83. Jock McAvoy
84. Eduardo Lausse
85. Eder Jofre
86. Charley Burley
87. Mike McCallum
88. Salvador Sanchez
89. Roy Jones Jr.
90. Rodolfo Gonzalez
91. Nigel Benn
92. (Irish) Bob Murphy
93. Paul Berlenbach
94. Battling Torres
95. Chalky Wright
96. George (KO) Chaney
97. Andy Ganigan
98. Fred Fulton
99. Ingemar Johansson
100. Charley White

Chapter Seven: The Top 20 Knockout Artists Of All Time

I have selected 20 individuals split across two eras in Boxing that I believe personify the absolute biggest punchers.

A great puncher is not always a great boxer but an individual who can deliver destruction and venom with their fists to destroy the opposition. It is always difficult to compare one era with another. What I would say is boxers have become bigger and stronger over time; better conditioned athletes, but I would also say technique has generally degraded and raw brute force has been the objective of training rather than springy and explosive power.

Would a Klitschko hit harder than a Marciano? Quite possibly but look at the height and weight difference! If Klitschko was 185 pounds and 5 feet 11 could he hit as hard as Rocky? Doubtful.

The earlier era goes from around 1920 to 1960. A big period that saw the Golden Age of boxing come into its own. New rules and regulations, including a limit of 20 rounds, also saw an evolution of technique and application of the sweet science. Arguably the superior all around fighters came from this period - people were generally far tougher and far hungrier.

The second modern era covers an even bigger timeline from 1960 to current day. This saw the sport become televised. No longer were the massive outdoor gates where the money was made. The impact on boxing was detrimental, as people stopped watching local amateur and pro boxing in person and instead watched championship fights from their living room. Think of the option of watching a Sunday league football game in person or a Premier League game on Sky. Less opportunities for boxers to breakthrough made for a smaller talent pool and loss of technique and skill in the sport.

I recall at 13 years old the excitement of watching live Mike Tyson Vs Michael Spinks on the 27th June 1987. It was a huge fight and a global event, of course a quick event when Tyson KO'd possibly the most frightened fighter I'd ever seen within one round. This fight was historic though because it was the last of the free heavyweight fights on tv, pay per view was born.

Big fights began to have tremendous build up periods and fighters began to avoid other top fighters in order to 'preserve records'. They fought less often and demonstrated less skill. Huge promoters made millions by splitting weight classes further and further and creating more and more organisations. Eight potential world champions at any given time had gone up to over one hundred.

In the modern-day tactics have changed, the champions have become more defensive and prefer to run and avoid than demonstrate great offensive skill. Was boxing not always supposed to be about winning by domination? Even Anthony Joshua, who is a big puncher and worthy Heavyweight Champion, in his rematch with Andy Ruiz Jr employed these tactics. Great fighters and contests do still exist, but they are far less common. The combat sport of MMA has also had a negative impact on Boxing. Fans have flocked to watch 'real' fighters going toe to toe with far less of the politics and fight records at stake. This has also resulted in the death of the local boxing clubs, once seen as the way out of poverty for talented, hungry and aggressive youngsters. The clubs have been dying a slow death for years whilst the MMA, BJJ and cage fighting fraternity open more and more clubs and recruit youngsters.

Despite all this there is still hope and particularly in the UK post the 2012 London Olympic games - a renaissance of young talent that came through the ranks has resulted in the most interesting heavyweight division for decades from 2020 onwards. One can only hope we can attract more youngsters and recreate some of the finest technique and skill of the old fighters to match the modern day science.

Top 10 Punchers in the Golden Age

1. Bob Fitzsimmons
2. Sam Langford
3. Jimmy Wilde
4. Jack Dempsey
5. Archie Moor
6. Sandy Sadler
7. Sugar Ray Robinson
8. Joe Louis
9. Rocky Marciano
10. Sonny Liston

Top 10 Punchers in the Modern Era

1. Joe Frazier
2. Earnie Shavers
3. George Foreman
4. Thomas Hearns
5. Marvin Hagler
6. Roberto Duran
7. Mike Tyson
8. Roy Jones Jnr
9. Anthony Joshua
10. Deontay Wilder

Bob Fitzimmons
Record: 89 wins (79 KOs) / 12 Losses
Style: Boxer Puncher
Signature Technique: Fitzsimmons shift
Famous KO: Round 14 KO James J. Corbett

"The bigger they are the harder they fall"
Bob Fitzsimons

The "Freckled Wonder," who mastered the art of delivering incredibly devastating power shots. A ferocious body puncher, his astonishing power helped him to capture the Middleweight title, Heavyweight title and then moved back down to win the Light Heavyweight title, becoming the first triple crown champion.

Bob Fitzsimmons made boxing history by becoming the sport's first three-division world champion, also holding the Guinness world record for being the lightest heavyweight champion.

Born in Cornwall on May 26, 1863, he was the youngest of seven boys and five girls. Before entering the world of professional boxing, Fitzsimmons briefly dabbled in a constellation of careers, working as a carriage painter, a butcher's delivery boy, a striker at an iron foundry, a decorator as well as an apprentice at his family's blacksmith forge. Throughout his life Fitzsimmons lived in several countries, including New Zealand, Australia and America. In his prime he stood 5ft 11ins and weighed 12 stone. He was very tall, slim and an explosive puncher. He was boxing's first triple-crown champion gaining the world's middleweight (1891-1897), light-heavyweight (1903-1905) and heavy-weight (1897-1899).

He had shoulders like a heavyweight and a vicious punch to match. He was strategic, crafty and very clever. He knew how to feint and draw his opponents

It is impossible to discuss knock out artists without discussing the power of Bob Fitzsimmons. Infamously he fought and knocked out seven men over nineteen rounds in one evening! Even more incredible is each weighed over 200 pounds - one was 6 foot 7 and 240 pounds! He was effectively a middleweight who fought heavy weights and destroyed them. His knowledge of anatomy and vital points allowed him to strike with pinpoint accuracy and stunning knockout power.

There are many interesting facts surrounding Fitz alongside his mysterious knock out power. As British he was celebrated at home but he never once fought professionally in the UK; only Australia, New Zealand and America. He perfected his hitting style by watching and studying the bare-knuckle champions that were still around then. He also strongly supported the practice of specific breathing exercises similar to Chinese chi gung to develop his power.

Fitz's fights were never short of drama, he once knocked out the original Jack Dempsey then continued to carry him to his corner! Fitz was also tried and acquitted on manslaughter charges when his sparring partner Con Riordan was knocked unconscious then died. When he beat Jim Corbett for the heavyweight title by 14th round KO it was the first boxing fight to be filmed in its entirety and the first fight to be reported on by a woman, Nellie Verrill.

The Fitzsimmons Shift

This won Fitz the world heavyweight championship against Corbett, in his own words: 'Feint with your right to your opponent's head. As you do so, step well in with your right foot, sneaking it in without his being aware; then send in a hard-left jab to the solar plexus. I would advise bringing it up in a short-left uppercut after landing on the mark.'

The strong reverse of legs and shoulders puts a huge amount of weight and force into the body jab. Almost 100 years later a young Mike Tyson was also regularly knocking people out with this very same shift and punch.

"I consider Bob Fitzsimmons as one of the greatest exponents of straight hitting that the prize ring has ever known. Fitz was a wonderful fighter and all of his straight punches were very effective. Until age set in and his hands went back on him, there were few fighters able to withstand that famous shift of his. When Fitz delivered a blow he carried the whole weight of his body with it."
Joe Gans

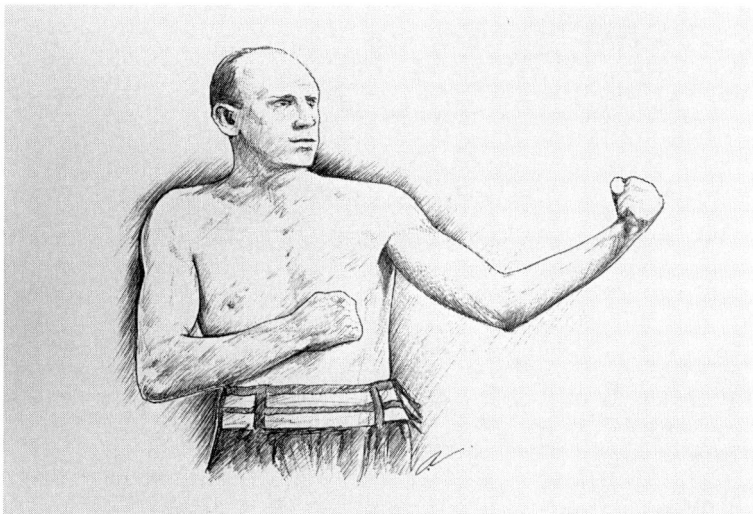

Above: Bob Fitzsimmons

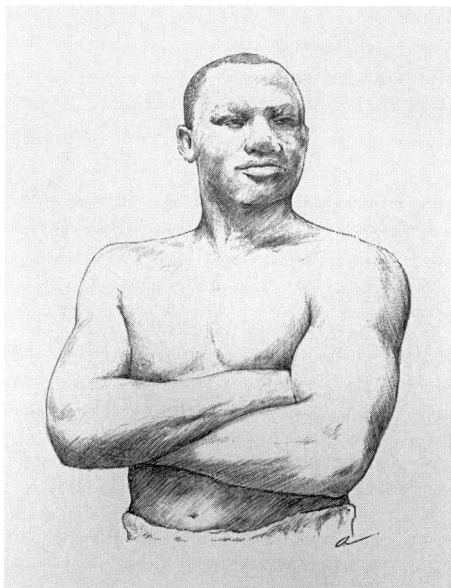

Left: Sam Langford

Sam Langford
Record: 211 wins (126 KOs) / 43 Losses
Style: Slugger/ Boxer Puncher
Signature Technique: Left Hook
Famous KO: Round 14 KO Harry Wills

"You'll pardon me gentlemen if I make the fight short. I have a train to catch."
Sam Langford

'Let me tell you that Sam Langford hit harder by accident than most heavy-weights did on purpose. There never lived a hitter like Langford.
Harry Wills

Sam Langford was known as the "Boston Terror" and "The Boston Tar Baby,". He is the most avoided fighter in history and therefore commonly known as the greatest fighter to never win a world championship. Standing only 5'6 and weighing 180 pounds he has more knockouts on his record than Mike Tyson and George Foreman combined.

His build was short and stocky with long arms and heavily muscled shoulders and back. As a technical puncher he was superb and could knock opponents out at both long and short range, he also had tremendous hand speed. With a solid chin and perfect balance and timing he was a phenomenal boxer and knock out artist supreme.The man nobody wanted to fight, with more knockouts recorded in boxing history than anyone else.

Sam Langford is a fighter you may never have heard of but really should have. He was never given the chance to even fight for a world title, partly due to racial discrimination and partly because nobody wanted to fight him. The Boston Tar Baby was an extremely strong, stocky fighter with incredible boxing ability and punching power. Although a natural middleweight Sam scored knockouts over nearly all the top heavyweights of his time (with the exception of Dempsey who would not fight him.)

During the mid-point of his career Langford developed severe eye-sight issues and was declared blind in 1930. He would fight his opponents on the inside so he could use touch to gauge where their arms were, at the end of the round he would need to use the ropes to find his way back to his corner. When he was half blind, he approached Jack Kearns the manager of World Heavyweight Champion Jack Dempsey and asked for a shot at the title, Kearns replied "Sam we were looking for somebody easier"

Langford's signature punch was the left hook for which was absolutely deadly for a man of his small size. He would add weight into the punch with a series of small foot shifts and he would shift his whole body to his right for in-creased force and hit straight through his opponent. He could deliver the punch from any angle and would often follow up with a right hand that was generally not needed.

Harry Wills has described what his KO's were like at the hands of Langford . Wills said of being hit: "I was knocked out three times in my career, twice by Langford and in my last fight by Paulino Uzcudun. I still don't know, except from hearsay, what punches Sam used to knock me out. The first time it happened was 1914. We were supposed to go twenty rounds, when the four-teenth began I was going easy. Sam was in a bad way. I backed him around the ring trying to set him up for a one punch finish. His eye was bleeding and the last thing I remember was having him against the ropes just about five feet from his corner. It must have happened right then."

"Two years later we were scheduled for another twenty rounder. In the eigh-teenth Sam was in a peck of trouble and once again I tried to set him up for a quick knockout. He finished the round okay and when the bell sounded for the start of the nineteenth, I was after him again. I figured if I could get him in a cor-ner, I could finish the fight. That was all I could remember. He must have caught me as I rushed in." The Feb 13, 1916 New Orleans Times-Picayune said it was "Langford's mighty left hook." Wills stated, "I don't know how long I was uncon-scious, but it must have been quite a while. He was marvellous as a fighting man; I'd venture to say unbeatable in his prime."

Sam Langford's Left Hook.

Sam's punching was made heavier because he knew how to use foot shifts to get maximum power into every punch, his left hook was his most dead-ly weapon, although he had many others. He could hit tremendously hard for his size. He would often feint to the body, two sometimes three times to trick the opponent then suddenly shoot the left hook to the jaw to the exposed dropped guard of his opponent. He would shift his weight to the right leg to deliver max-imum force. He could deliver this punch from various angles normally followed through with the right hand though it was seldom needed!

The great Jack Dempsey wrote in his autobiography "there was one man I wouldn't fight because I knew he would flatten me; I was afraid of Sam Langford".

Jimmy Wilde – The Ghost With The Hammer In His Hand
Record: 149 wins (99 KOs) / 3 Losses
Style: Slugger/Boxer Puncher
Signature Technique: Big right hand
Famous KO: Round 11 Young Zulu Kidd

"In America they had no chance - I knocked them all cold in America"
Jimmy Wilde

Most boxing historians consider Jimmy Wilde to be pound for pound the hardest puncher of all time. The first and greatest flyweight champion weighed around 100 pounds (he was sometimes mistaken for a child!), but it wasn't unusual for him to knock out men twice his size earning him the nicknames the 'mighty atom' and the 'ghost with the hammer in his hand.' He had incredible strength, timing, balance, speed and precision.
Wilde maintains a 93-bout unbeaten run, which is a record that stands to this day and it is unlikely to ever be beaten. As he began boxing prior to any records it has been estimated that he is likely to have fought several times per day and over 800 times in his entire career.
Born in Wales and working in the coal mines from the age of 14, he had developed not only strong shoulders but a toughness and resilience to match. Wilde had a unique boxing style at that time - to hold his hands low and sway side to side firing in punches from all angles. He was mentored by the legendary Jim Driscoll who he learned his technical skills from such as parrying, feinting and footwork, but he was a natural born hitter.
Wilde was powerful beyond belief and without any fear to step into the ring against much bigger and heavier men. Bouncing on the balls of his feet, his hands often at his waist, he would strike with lightning speed and launch his most dangerous weapon, the big right hand. It was a mystery to many how a man so tiny could hit so hard. He was noted to have an almost sixth sense; the ability to anticipate his opponent's next move and beat him to it. Wilde was a highly skilled boxer and the power of his punches was almost magical. Wilde had an incredible sense of distance, able to avoid blows by an inch or two and fire back cleanly in exchange. He was never off his toes with his knees bent and constantly moving. An extremely difficult man to face and lights out if he hit you.

"Jimmy was the greatest fighter I ever saw."
Gene Tunney

Above: Jack Dempsey

Left: Jimmy Wilde

Jack Dempsey – Savagery In Motion
Record: 54 wins (44 KOs) / 6 Losses
Style: Slugger/In fighter
Signature Technique: Dempsey Triple
Famous KO: Round 3 TKO Jess Willard

'A good fighter must have many qualities. First comes top physical condition. No fighter should enter ring combat unless he knows he's physically fit. He must be able to take and give a good punch. Speed is another essential. He should be able to work rapidly with his hands and be able to move about in a position from which he can both strike and avoid being hit. He must like to fight. Keeping his weight within the requirements of his class is also essential. If one is a Heavyweight, weight doesn't count so much as in other divisions, so long as one doesn't become flabby and slow down. A top Heavyweight should possess speed, punching power, plus the ability to take a good punch. Slow-moving fighters are useless. They can make no progress. They are impeded by their movements.'
Jack Dempsey

Jack Dempsey was heavyweight champion from1919 to 1926. He was a highly aggressive brawler who weighted around 185 pounds but had exceptional explosive power and hands as fast as lightning. Innovative technique-wise, he used clever footwork and stance switches together with great head movement.

The Manassa Mauler has and always will be a puncher's favourite, and a stunning knock out artist. Although he was not infallible, as proven by Gene Tunney who was a masterful defensive and strategic boxer. Dempsey had a rock solid punch, an unstoppable toughness and a scientific method of mechanics which underpinned his savagery. He even wrote a book - 'Championship Fighting – explosive punching and aggressive defence', which set the standard for heavy punching and more than 50 years later is still THE go to book for mechanics in boxing and indeed any striking art.

Dempsey knew how to hit hard on every single blow he threw. He was fierce, aggressive, unique at that time. The Dempsey style on the surface comprised of bobbing and weaving and an onslaught of hooks and straights to body and head. His attack was his defence; the bobs and weaves kept the head off the line and the low crouched posture, leaning into every punch, added clever angles to miss incoming punches. Dempsey was also remarkably fast for a heavyweight and could take a punch. His dynamic encounter with Louis Firpo saw him being clean knocked out of the ring before coming back to claim victory.

Dempsey named four key principles in his punching mechanics:

1. The falling step – transferring weight from rear to front leg through inertia
2. The leg spring – forward exploding momentum.
3. The shoulder whirl – a quick and full rotation of the shoulders by pulling on the opposite shoulder as the punch begins, timed with weight transfer.
4. The upward surge – driving vertical force into uppercut punches.

When Dempsey first came on the scene he was seen as very unique and different. For a time, his style was named as the American style, which was dramatically different from the clean, stylish, pinpoint accurate old English style. Let us take a look at some of the characteristics of this 'new style' that emerged with this notorious fighter:

*   A deep bent stance. This is both defensive to keep the body away from harm but also acts like a spring to compress and store energy in the body prior to explosive release. For a tall fighter it is not advisable to adopt this as they will be losing their natural height and reach advantage and bringing their head down to the opponent. There needs to be some distance between the feet for balance and stability.

*   Generally, the hands are kept high and the chin well down to avoid stepping in to blows as this is a forward charging style. At times Dempsey would deliberately drop his hands. A particular favourite 'cheeky tactic' was to squat low and hold both hands on his thighs. This was an invitation to the party and the door swung open to a hard body hook.

*   Bobbing and weaving. The swinging of the head left and right is governed by the punches being thrown. When you throw a hard right hook the body swings over to the left, with a left hook it swings to the right. This maximises the weight and force into each blow and confuses the opponent who finds it difficult to hit the head, particularly if they are not used to facing this style, it can throw all their calculations and distancing off course.

*   Footwork. Along with the bobbing and weaving the feet must be constantly on the move; short sliding steps cutting up the ring and finding new angles. This creates unpredictability and opportunity to gain advantage, and added protection from adapting an aggressive defense.

Common punches and combinations in the Dempsey style:

*   Left hook to the body followed by a right hook to the other side.
*   Left hook to the body followed by left hook.

• Right hook to the body followed by right hook to the head.

The Dempsey Triple

This was Jack's signature move and he often used the same combination of three blows to finish off the opponent. From a left lead, step in with the right foot and hook a hard right to the body directly under the opponent's heart as you duck to the left, rapidly follow this punch with a left hook to the same point as you duck to the right and finally rise up and finish with a right hook to the jaw.

To maximise these punches the feet must work alongside the hands and be in the correct position. In the first right punch, it must be combined and timed correctly with the right (rear) leg stepping forward and leaning the body to the left. Step forward on the left foot for the left punch and lean to the right for the final punch, rise up on your toes and pivot towards the opponent.

Finally, a point about Dempsey's style; it is definitely not for everyone. The fighter should be naturally aggressive and always moving forward and also have tremendous fitness as there is no pause or let up in this style; you will be throwing punches from beginning to end.

The Dempsey Triple

Archie Moore - 'The Old Mongoose'
Record: 186 wins (131 KOs) / 23 Losses
Style: Boxer-puncher
Signature Technique: Fake cross – lead hook
Famous KO: Archie Moore vs Yvon Durelle I

'Nobody's been stronger than me in there. The fella might be bigger, heavier.
But he ain't any stronger.'
Archie Moore

Archie Moore was a pure "boxer-puncher" he was superior from
both being in the clinch and from a long distance where he circled around his
opponents using his jab. He liked to use angles and stance switches and was
very technical but had an undeniable level of knockout power. Moore holds the
record for the most knockouts in boxing history. He fought for 27 years as a top
contender and was a light-heavyweight champion for nearly 10 years, winning
the title at 39 years of age and retaining it until he was 48.

Moore, real name Archibald Lee Wright was born in Benoit, Mississippi
in 1916. A natural athlete who found himself at reform school for petty theft. He
soon began to train in the school's gym and took part in amateur bouts during
his time inside the institution that ultimately turned his life around. Whilst competing on the amateur circuit he was employed doing forestry work which gave
him a tremendous physique, strength and overall fitness.

As a young professional he travelled the country for fights and even
went to Australia where he beat the best over there in 7 contests. His career
almost ended when a perforated ulcer required major surgery, he also caught
pneumonia and went down to less than 100 pounds in weight. He was told he
wouldn't box again but had other ideas himself. He built himself back up and
even used a car license plate as protective cover over his healing scar so he
could spar. After being denied chances at the title due to his colour he went to
Argentina and had eight fights, winning seven and drawing one.

At the age of 36, having spent seventeen years as a pro boxer and after 128 bouts, he was given a chance and won the light heavyweight title. After
several defences he decided to step up to heavyweight and challenge Rocky
Marciano. Marciano had 49 consecutive victories and was 7 years younger than
Moore, and was 4-1 odds favourite to win. Moore lost in the 9th round by KO
but had dropped Marciano in the 2nd for the first time in his career.

Moore continued to be the king of the light heavyweight division for
over a decade. His final career loss was to his former apprentice Cassius Clay.
Archie Moore had a somewhat busy retirement as a trainer, working with and
developing many young professionals including a certain George Foreman.

Archie Moore will always be remembered as an incredibly talented
fighter with exceptional knockout power. His career spanned over four decades

at the top level, which was a testament to his technical skill and ability. He was old school and one of the best ever.

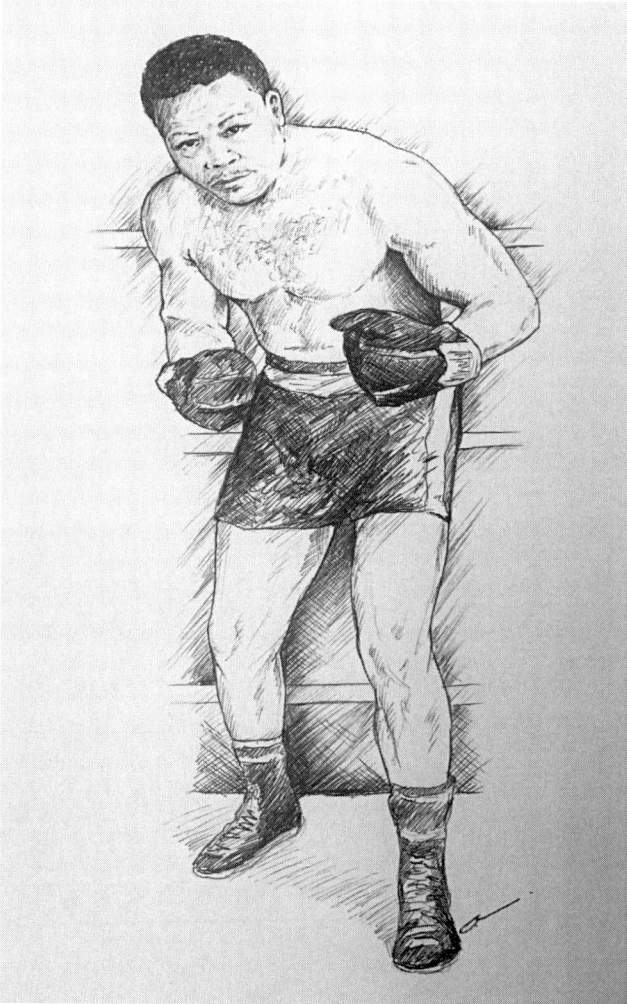

Archie Moore

Sandy Sadler
Record: 145 wins (104 KOs) / 16 Losses
Style: Slugger
Signature Technique: Gazelle Left Hook
Famous KO: Round 4 Willie Pep

"I thought I fought a clean fight"
Sandy Sadler

Born Joseph Saddler, 'Sandy' Saddler is perhaps both the greatest featherweight and the greatest junior lightweight in the history of boxing. Somewhat of a freak standing at 5'8 and a half with a 70-inch reach, which is as long as many heavyweights. He was tall and skinny - lanky but a vicious slugger with ridiculous power, particularly demonstrated in his with leaping left hook. Like an earlier version of Thomas Hearns, he liked to also fire off a stiff jab followed by a right hand from the depths of hell.

As an amateur Saddler fought 50 bouts losing only 3 or 4 times. He started young as a professional at 17 and initially did not have a great start after losing two of his first ten contests. However, in his second year as a professional he won 14 consecutive fights by KO, with seven occurring in the first round. He was quickly becoming a fighter to avoid and it was after some 94 fights that he was given a shot at the title against Willie Pep. Saddler KO'd the great Pep in the fourth round much to the surprise of many. Pep took the rematch on points, altogether they fought 4 times, Saddler won 3-1 with all three victories by knockout.

The fourth and final Pep vs Saddler contest saw both fighters suspended for 6 months by the New York State boxing commission. Even world heavyweight champion Rocky Marciano, whose was not exactly the cleanest of fighters, called the contest "the roughest, dirtiest fight I have ever seen". Both fighters gouged, butted, wrestled and even tried to strangle one another.

In the sands of time Saddler has perhaps been eclipsed by Pep in terms of legacy and greatness, which seems unfair seeing as he beat him three out of four times. It has been said though that Pep was not in his prime. Regardless, Pep was the peoples champion and the majority seem to prefer his graceful dancing defensive style to the vicious punching battering ram that Sadler was. Maybe such savagery is not as pleasing to the eye as other styles, but in realm of knockout artists we salute Saddler as one of the all-time greatest.

A final fact on Sandy, his brother named his son Joseph after him. That nephew Joseph Saddler grew up to be the legendary hip hop DJ, Grandmaster Flash. Joseph "Sandy" Sandler the fighter was a king among big punchers with his monstrous power and the greatest Featherweight in boxing history.

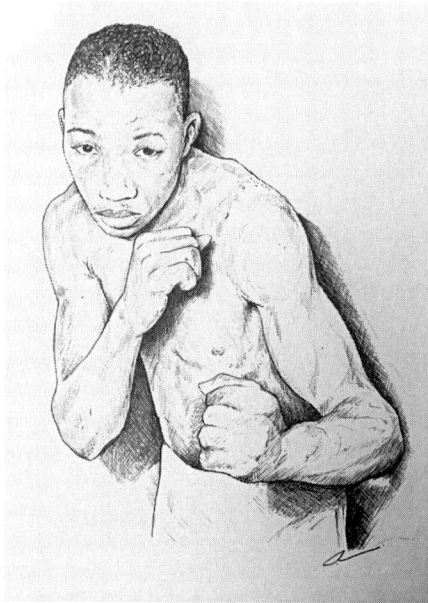

Left: Sandy Sadler

Right: Sugar Ray Robinson

Sugar Ray Robinson – The Most Complete Boxer
Record: 173 wins (109 KOs) / 19 Losses
Style: Boxer Puncher
Signature Technique: Left hook
Famous KO: Jake LaMotta Round 13 TKO

Rhythm is everything in boxing. Every move you make starts with your heart, and that's in rhythm or you're in trouble. Your rhythm should set the pace of the fight. If it does, then you penetrate your opponent's rhythm. You make him fight your fight, and that's what boxing is all about."
Sugar Ray Robinson

Widely recognised as the greatest of all time and the most complete boxer, Sugar Ray was 2x Ring Magazine Fighter of the Year (1942 & 1951), 5x Middleweight World Champion and 2x Weight World Champion. The absolute master of the sweet science. Muhammad Ali called him 'The king, the master, my idol.

Flawless technique, timing and speed, combined with exceptional reflexes and nonstop explosive power make him the most fundamentally complete boxer who threw the most perfect punches. Sugar Ray's era was full of legendary boxers and he beat them all - Jake La Motta, Gene Fullmer, Henry Armstrong, Carmen Basilio, Bobo Olson, Kid Gavilan, and Rocky Graziano. Sugar Ray fought for over 25 years at top class level, at the end of his career his face was unmarked and still as handsome, in his prime he went on an undefeated run of 91 fights.

At 12 years old he went into a boxing gymnasium and was trained in the old school by George Gainsford. He made his amateur debut standing in for a boy who was unfit and went on, like many of the greats, to be a Golden Gloves Champion before he became the King of the welterweights. Completely dedicated to the science of boxing he even studied human anatomy to improve the delivery of his venomous punches.

Here are six signature skills that made Sugar Ray Robinson the greatest of all time, the most complete fighter that ever lived and a top tier knockout artist:

1. Footwork
   Sugar Ray's footwork, and indeed foot speed and agility, is what enabled his punches to be so powerful and accurate, it carried him through his 25 years at the top and required extreme fitness and conditioning.
   Ray's lateral movement around the clock gave him both defence and elusiveness but also impossible angles to shoot punches from. He was the source of the Ali shuffle and everything seen in the classy footwork of boxers like Muhammed Ali. Sugar Ray Leonard was named after him.

2. Hand Speed

    If in boxing we say speed kills, then in this case Sugar Ray Robinson was a mass murderer. His superior speed facilitated his jabs and power shots to rarely miss, and produce tremendous force.

    The kind of speed Ray could produce was partly genetic from his natural athletic ability but also a result of the relentless old school conditioning methods and training he implemented. He was never out of shape and his speed was with him right up to the end of his career.

3. The Body Jab

    Sugar Ray knew to work the body to open the head, his use of body jab-bing, often with a stiff arm, was perfection. Not only did this tire and work down his opponents but it also acted as an antenna or range finder to put him in perfect position to unleash right hand strikes. The mechanics of the set up enabled him to throw his whole body into the following punch.

    Sugar Ray Leonard emulated his namesake in this aspect as did many oth-er modern day boxers such as Floyd Mayweather Jnr. The only difference being the these two modern emulators, as great as they were, never had Robinsons knock out power. Once the opponent begins to worry about that body jab they are in perfect position to receive the KO punch.

4. Punches in Bunches

    Sugar Ray's high knockout rate against the highest level of competition was due to his ability to throw undulating smooth nonstop combinations. This was seen in his punishing encounters with Jake LaMotta, who was often in a state of confusion as to where punches would come from next. He doubled and tripled straights, hooks and uppercuts in different rhythms and combinations.

    With his signature hairstyle flopping left right and centre, Ray had venom in every single punch, which were perfectly delivered from every single angle imaginable. Again, a fighter from the modern era such as Roy Jones Jnr took inspiration from Ray's style.

    Sugar Ray Robinson is in a class of his own in combination punching - the best combination puncher ever. His accuracy, variety and unpredictable patterns of combinations made his punches impossible to defend against for his opponents.

5. The Left Hook

    The left hook of Sugar Ray Robinson came with a serious health warning and it is no surprise that it became known as the 'perfect punch' after a 5th round KO of Gene Fullmer in 1957, who said:

    "It supposedly was the greatest left hook he ever threw, and it happened to hit me on the chin, when I came to, I was standing up and he was stand-ing in the other corner jumping up and down. I asked my manager, I said, 'How come Robinson is doing exercises between rounds?' He said, 'It's not between rounds.' I said, 'What do you mean?' He said, 'They counted 10.'

I said, 'It must've been me because I never heard any of it."
The majority of fighters expect punches to be thrown in a chain sequence such as right, left, right, left. Ray could double up or even tripled up on his left hook, which was revolutionary at that time.

6. The Right Kidney Hook

A signature Punch Ray used in virtually all of his fights. One of Ray Robinson's signature shots was once an opponent presented Ray with their back, he would corkscrew his right hand around their sides and into their kidneys. He was even disqualified for using it against the German fighter Gerhard Hecht.

This punch is unpredictable, Ray would fire his jab high immediately dropping low to launch a wide right hook. He stepped into the left with it and turned it over to keep his thumb pointing at the floor weaving his full body weight to the lead left leg. An absolute vicious and showstopper.

'There's too much violence in the world, most of it perpetrated on me by Sugar Ray Robinson. I came at that guy with a vengeance. He came at me with punches. Robinson opened everything I had that was closed, and closed everything that was open. But there was one thing you could say about me as a fighter—I kept my head. I lost my teeth, but I kept my head.'
Jake LaMotta

Joe Louis - Perfection
Record: 66 wins (52 KOs) / 3 Losses
Style: Boxer Puncher
Signature Technique: Straight Right
Famous KO: Round 1 KO Max Schmeling

"There is no such thing as a natural boxer. A natural dancer has to practice hard. A natural painter has to paint all the time. Even a natural fool has to work at it."
Joe Louis

Few people would argue that Joe Louis the 'Brown Bomber' was not the best boxer there ever was. He certainly has to be in everyone's top three. His strengths we will examine later, but it is impossible to name a weakness. As a young professional he was mentored by Jack Blackburn who taught him strong fundamentals, which led to his style being almost so minimalistic that it led to perfection. Personality-wise he was as cool as a cucumber without a hint of anger but be under no illusion his fists were loaded with dynamite and he had incredible amounts of power.

In his own words:
"Correct punching demands careful study and practice to perfect. Powerful punching does not derive from just the hands and arms; but from the body when properly used. Use the weight of your body in every punch, and the arms as a transmitter. Punching straight from the shoulder means the weight shifted so that the hips and shoulder lead the arm to the centre of the object."

Those fists knocked out the best heavyweights of that time including former champions Primo Carnera and Max Baer. In 1937 he became world heavyweight champion by knocking out the Cinderella man James J Braddock in the eighth round, it wasn't an easy ride as he pulled himself up from the canvas in round one. He then had a five-year undefeated streak of 21 fights before he served as sergeant instructor during World War two. After the war he had four more defences before retirement. As usual with many fighters, financial issues caused him to return to the ring and make a comeback. He won eight fights but then lost by KO in the eighth round of his last fight to a much younger Rocky Marciano.

Joe Louis' record, ability and overall career easily crown him the best of the best. But to really appreciate his greatness one has to examine his skill and technique as a boxing genius, which is why he is perfection. He always held his guard high, elbows in and kept his chin down. He threw short range and precise punches and never wasted any energy. He could throw a five or six punch combination with ridiculous power. Fighters like Jack Johnson,

Muhammad Ali and Tyson Fury box to keep their opponent away and off of them so they could score points from outside. Louis boxed his way in to get close so he could unleash hell and knock their block off.

Jack Blackburn had schooled him in the art of drawing to attack instead of reaching. Every great knock out artist knows you can hit an opponent harder and cleaner if they are moving towards you, than if they are moving away. Louis would sneakily edge towards an opponent and then make a small step back drawing them into him. It was like a spider's web, when the opponent entered into range he would step in and unleash his short quick shots with massive impact. Some thought this meant he was too static, flat footed and had poor footwork. This could not be further from the truth. He had perfect footwork for the boxer puncher he was, which was to go on the attack and not run. Louis' balance was incredible, never compromised and allowed him to use full body-weight in his punches.

Louis was also a master at cutting the ring off and placing the opponent right where he wanted them. He would also confused them as to what he was doing and what would hit them next. He was expert at parrying and feinting to create the gaps he wanted to fire in his missiles.

He wasn't a pressure infighter like a Tyson, Dempsey or Frazier. Louis preferred instead to stalk his prey and set up their demise. Like a frog in boiling water, this was subtle and often the opponent did not realise the danger he was in until it was too late. Louis was always in control and dictated the pace and outcome of his fights. He could fight equally well on the inside or the outside, once his opponent was in the danger zone, he handed them a swift and brutal death sentence. Louis absolutely combined power, brawn, technique and skill with brains. That is why he was perfect.

Joe Louis had the complete set, he had everything. Dempsey and Marciano were great punchers but lacked Louis's hand speed. Frazier and Tyson had similar speed, but neither could put punches together in combination as precise, accurate and deadly as Louis did. Joe also had amazing stamina and conditioning. He was as dangerous in round one as round twelve, he never faded, lost power or dropped his impeccably perfect form. If you were to look up 'boxer puncher' in the dictionary it should simply have a picture of Joe Louis.

'There's never been a boxer better than Joe Louis. You'd take one shot from him and you were sure he'd have seven or eight more coming for you. Certainly, Muhammad Ali was the greatest man ever to fight, but not the greatest boxer.'
George Foreman

'I used to tease Joe Louis by reminding him that I was the greatest of all time. But Joe Louis was the greatest heavyweight fighter ever.'
Muhammad Ali

'I define fear as standing across the ring from Joe Louis and knowing he wants to go home early.'
Max Baer

'Joe Louis, to me, was the finest human being God put on this earth in every way.'
Angelo Dundee

'Joe Louis is the greatest heavyweight champion of all time.'
Joe Frazier

'Every time I hear the name Joe Louis my nose starts to bleed.'
Tommy Farr

'When you're a great finisher, you'll become popular. Joe Louis was a great finisher.'
Mike Tyson

'He was a credit to his race – the human race.'
Jimmy Cannon

Above: Rocky Marciano

Left: Joe Louis

Rocky Marciano – Unbeaten Perfect Record
Record: 49 wins (43 KOs) / 0 Losses
Style: Slugger
Signature Technique: Overhand right (Suzie Q)
Famous KO: Round 8 Ezzard Charles

'Basically, my style was always my own. I pressed. Once you get a guy in the corner, he has nowhere to go.'
Rocky Marciano

Rocco Francis Marchegiano was born to poor Italian parents on 1 September 1923 and almost lost his first battle with pneumonia at the age of 19 months. After being drafted into the army in 1943 the story goes that he knocked out an Australian in a pub in Cardiff, it was to be the first of many knockouts. His first love was baseball, but boxing was his future, he was disqualified in his first amateur fight after he kneed his opponent in the groin because he felt too tired to hold his hands up.

Luckily, he managed to get himself in good enough condition to start a professional career in 1947. Not that he needed to worry about his cardio too much because in the first two years his fights never lasted more than three rounds. Despite beating 22 opponents in 62 rounds the famous boxing manager somewhat reluctantly took him on. Weighing 184 pounds and at 5'11 with short arms and flat feet he was seen as far from an ideal Heavyweight contender.

A champion he was soon to be though, after ending Joe Louis's career by an eight round knockout. After making quick work of Lee Savold and Harry 'Kid' Matthews he finally got a shot at the Champion, Jersey Joe Walcott. Rocky had to pull himself up from the canvass for the first time in his career in the first round, he took considerable punishment but eventually put Jersey Joe down in the thirteenth. His forward pressing style of delivering punches from all angles imaginable had prevailed. For most boxers who had a rematch with Rocky, things usually got much worse second time around. This was no different for Walcott who was dispatched in the first round. Marciano had other notable wins, over Ezzard Charles (twice) Don Cockell and Archie Moore.

Following his retirement, he was one of the few fighters to really stay retired and he invested his money wisely. He sadly died in a plane crash just before his 46th Birthday, but his legacy is still with us. He is still the only heavyweight champion to remain unbeaten with a perfect record of 49-0. He was Ring Magazine Fighter of the year three times and also won fight of the year three times. In 2000 Ring Magazine also voted Rocky the ninth greatest fighter of the twentieth century among all weight classes.

It has been said that Marciano's impeccable record was aided by the division being weak and him fighting aging fighters. It was actually a far stronger division than anything that followed for the next 40 years. He fought and beat great fighters. His knockout ratio was 88% compared to Joe Louis's 76%. He had absolutely devasting power in his fists, he trained seriously was never out of shape and was basically built to knock people out. He often fought fighters 30 or 40 pounds heavier than himself (and did better against the bigger one's). He had the shortest reach of any heavyweight ever yet the most stunning one punch knock out power.

Rocky famously said "Why waltz 10 rounds with an opponent if you can KO him in one?"

Rocky has been wrongly accused of being a wild, swinging and crude boxer. However, he knew the sweet science and the secrets of knock out power through physics and body mechanics. He was a 184-pound man that could hit harder than a 250 pound man.

Set up

Rocky knew how to set himself when he delivered his punches. A pure boxer stylist will often be on their toes, mobile, with little contact with the floor when they hit. The force of his impact comes from his arms and shoulders only. But a slugger such as Joe Louis, Dempsey, Frazier, Foreman, Tyson, or Marciano, will plant their feet flat as he punches, using the floor for leverage to get more of his body weight behind the punch.

Commitment

Marciano was never a fighter who worried about a counter blow, he never held back through fear of retaliation, he accepted that he might get hit in return and couldn't care less. Rocky put everything into the punch. He accepted that by stepping into the ring he would get hit a lot during the course of a fight. He accepted it beforehand so it never came into the equation of 100% intensity into every punch. When Rocky let go he was totally committed, putting every ounce of energy and body weight into every punch.

Ground Force

The power for Rocky began in his feet when he pushed off the ground. Kinetic energy was transferred by his thick truck like legs, through his hip and then by the twist of his upper body as he snapped his arm and fist through the target. Rocky's force was equal to the mass of the arm plus the weight of his body that he moved forward as he stepped.

Close Range

Like Louis, Marciano's punches were close range. As the arm moves forward the time from beginning to end increases as you increase the distance of the thrown punch. Since velocity = distance per time, that means the longer the range the less velocity. If the punch is shorter, traveling only a few inches, your velocity will increase and the transmitted energy at impact far greater. Marciano gave a huge weight advantage away to opponents, but he would shuffle as close as he could get to the opponent, plant his legs and twist his body with maximum force as he stepped in. The result being all 184 pounds went into that punch as opposed to just arm power.

What boxers said of Marciano's punching power:

"It hurt to bump into him....He hits harder than Max Schmeling...this kid is tough enough to beat anyone."
"The Rock didn't know too much about the boxing book, but it wasn't a book he hit me with. It was a whole library of bone crushers."
Joe Louis

"Joe could take you out with combinations...Marciano was a one-punch artist. He threw every punch like you throw a baseball, as hard as he could. I have to say, with all respect to Joe, Marciano hit harder than Joe Louis."
Jersey Joe Walcott

"Rocky numbs you all over. Wherever he hits you, he hurts you; on the arms, the shoulders, the neck and the head."
Ezzard Charles

"After a fight with Marciano, it felt like you had been beat all over the upper body with a blackjack or hit with rocks. He could hurt you, sure, but it was the quantity of his punches. He just had more stamina than anyone else in those days. He was like a bull with gloves."
Archie Moore

"I would throw a hard punch, then he would throw a hard punch. The difference was that Rocky would throw 10 more. He just never stopped throwing punches."
Roland LaStarza

"He was a great puncher, one of the best of all-time. He just threw one punch after another, and all of them were hard."
Harry "Kid" Matthews

"He had amazing strength. Any time Marciano hit you, he could hurt you. He didn't do much flicking; every punch was a knockout punch."
Bernie Reynolds

"In the ring he looked sloppy and awkward sometimes, but that was deceptive because he was terribly strong, could punch and take a punch...Jersey Joe

Walcott had made him miss for twelve rounds and then Rocky took his title away in the thirteenth. Ezzard Charles seemed to be making him look bad, but Rocky busted up his face something horrible...I respected Marciano"
Floyd Patterson

"What everyone forgets is that Marciano can punch harder with a right hand than any modern-day heavyweight. In his first fight with Walcott, Rocky needed only one blow to win the title. The power in his right scrambled Jersey Joe's brains at Chicago."
"I've scored my share of knockouts along the way, but more often than not my opponents got up after being knocked down and had to be knocked down repeatedly. The same is true of Joe Louis. But Marciano needs only one solid smash and it's all over. That's why I say Rocky Marciano is the hardest-hitting heavyweight champion I have seen."
Jack Dempsey

Sonny Liston – The Most Feared Fighter
Record: 50 wins (39 KOs) / 4 Losses
Style: Slugger
Signature Technique: Jab
Famous KO: Round 1 Floyd Patterson

'I had nothing when I was a kid but a lot of brothers and sisters, a helpless mother and a father who didn't care about any of us. We grew up with few clothes, no shoes, little to eat. My father worked me hard and whupped me hard.'
Sonny Liston

The menace and coldness in the face of Charles 'Sonny' Liston no doubt contributed to his outstanding career as a world heavyweight champion and knockout artist par excellence. One of 25 children, he spent much of his youth on the wrong side of the law until he was locked up for armed robbery and had his energies channelled into the sweet science by a prison chaplain.

He turned professional shortly after winning a golden gloves tournament and had all the hall marks and gifts of a future champion. Liston was physically imposing. standing 6 feet 1 inch and 216 pounds. He had a gigantic reach of 84 inches, the second longest behind the mighty Primo Carnera. His 18-inch neck sat upon a heavily muscular torso and 'quad-zilla' legs. His whole-body power was channelled through massive fists measuring 15 inches in diameter. This was a dangerous man in many ways.

The only mark on his early boxing career was a points loss to Marty Marshall who had broken his jaw mid-way though the fight. On his way to meeting the Champion Floyd Patterson he eliminated, assassinated and destroyed every man in his way. Liston was never exactly the people's choice and made to wait by the powers that be due to his criminal record and somewhat less than poster boy image surrounding him. Rumours of involvement with the mafia persisted and it was generally accepted they had a hand in managing Liston.

Poor Floyd Patterson didn't stand a chance, Sonny bulldozed him into oblivion in round one with absolute savagery. The left hook that took him out lifted him off his feet and he never stood back up. The rematch ten months later was more of the same and again lasted only one round. Sonny Liston looked absolutely invincible.

Unfortunately, time was catching up with him and waiting to be champion had removed his best years at the top. A ten years younger, cocky, superfit young man named Cassius Clay challenged for the crown. Liston couldn't take him out and looked old and tired next to the vibrant Clay, he refused to come out for the 7th round after complaining of a shoulder injury. The rematch 1 year later was one of the most controversial boxing fights in history. Liston went down after one minute to a 'phantom' punch nobody saw. There were cries of fix;

nobody will ever know for sure except Sonny who sadly passed away in 1970 under very mysterious circumstances. A controversial character from beginning to end, he was always portrayed as the 'bad guy' that everyone loved to hate. Friends and family have spoken of a very different man in person who had a very gentle and kind heart; either way we celebrate this man as a stunning knock out artist.

Similar to the case of many other knock out artists and power punchers, Liston's technical skills are both overlooked and underrated as a result of his size and devastating strength. It is not possible to be such a dominating force in a division of that quality at that time without an elite level of skill and technique to match his power

'Sparring with Liston is the most dangerous thing that I ever did in my entire life. As I said earlier, no matter what I tried against him, it was me who had to revert back to boxing. Nobody made me box like Sonny Liston did and that happened every time we worked together. He taught me many things, including the importance of the jab. I just couldn't get mine straight and every day he had me working on it.

There were times when he could have knocked my head off but he didn't because we were pretty good friends. I saw the way he stared at people and I took on some of that behaviour to intimidate opponents. That was where some of that 'Bad George' came from, hanging around with Sonny.'
George Foreman

Sonny Liston was no clumsy out of control bully, he had a very classic and sweet boxing style. He did not lack speed, he could fire off a jab or left hook as quick as any heavyweight; power needs velocity, slow hands are weak. He did not waste energy on long combinations of flicking multiple jabs to set up a right. He was a heavy hard puncher, ncluding his jab, and his hooks were like bombs. Liston also had a decent defence with great head movement and positioning. He may not have been elegant or graceful in his movement, but he was knock out artist, he was far from stiff or mechanical and he knew how to dictate the pace of a fight and ultimately control it.

Sonny Liston's Jab

With great punchers we often look at the right hand, Liston had a terrifying right cross and left hook but he also had one of the best Jabs in history. Liston had multiple uses for his jab not just to hurt his opponent. He used the jab to control the pace of the fight, occupying his opponents' space and setting up his offence.

Liston's optimum range was the middle range. Here he was close enough to land big shots by planting his feet, but also far enough away to have space for extending his arms and to torque his body and arms into a punch. To keep this distance between him and the opponent, Liston stiffly stuck his lead hand in his opponent's face whenever they threatened to come forward. To extend the jab, he would lean his whole body into the punch. By pushing his shoulders forward, and leaning his torso into his opponent, he added inches onto his jab, keeping his opponent at the end of his fist.

Liston also liked to extend his jab out and momentarily leave it there. This disrupts the opponent's balance, forcing him to reset himself to regain balance control. Liston's pushing jab reasserted the distance between him and his opponent, leaving the opponent wondering how he can get into position to land his own power punches. Liston would like to keep his arm extended in his opponent's face, blinding his opponent. He used his extended lead hand to occupy his opponent space until he was in position to land the right hand. Liston would push his jab out, and then step in so that he didn't have to reach with the right hand. Being closer to his opponent, he could then simply turn his right side into the punch. This allowed him to generate more power in his legs more efficiently. Liston would also use the double jab, to set up his right hand. He would step into a new position whilst throwing the double jab, coming from a different angle. By stepping into his right side, he ends up on the outside of his opponent's lead left shoulder. This forced his opponent to make more of an effort to turn, if he plans to land his punch. This bought time for Liston to throw punches whilst his opponent readjusted.

In conclusion, Sonny Liston is highly underrated and lacking credit as a great boxer and monster puncher. He is definitely up there with the best and it is no wonder he was so feared.

"Before I met Sonny Liston I was known as an intimidator, but that guy was maybe the ultimate intimidator who ever lived. I had 16 amateur fights, won the golden gloves, had 52 pro fights, fought Ali, fought George Foreman, but no one hit me like that guy hit me. He broke my nose. Broke my cheekbone, I had to have 72 stitches after that fight. Everywhere he hit me he broke me".
"He was everything they said he was, a mass of muscles, power, force........."
Muhammed Ali

Above: Sonny Liston

Left: Joe Frazier

Joe Frazier – A Smokin' Gun
Record: 32 wins (27 KOs) / 4 Losses
Style: In fighter
Signature Technique: Left hook
Famous KO: Jimmy Ellis KO round 4

'The boxing writers would talk about the glee I showed when I took apart a guy. Why not? I came into the fight game marked down as damaged merchandise, as too small to operate against the big guys. Well, let me tell you; there wasn't a feeling much better than seeing the look in that big guy's eyes when I'd unload on them.'
Joe Frazier

Joe Frazier stood six feet tall, 210 pounds and legs like tree trunks, which supported him like the foundations of a building as he endlessly came forward bobbing and weaving from a low crouch in relentless fashion. He was elusive, hard to hit, aggressive and strong. Nobody had a left hook like Joe Frazier. He wore many quality top tier opponents down with his unique style and of course was the first man to defeat Muhammed Ali in what has been called the fight of the century over 50 years ago.

Born one of thirteen children to poor parents, he idolised Joe Louis as a kid and even built a punchbag out of hay so he could imitate his hero. In a Rocky-esque way he moved to Philadelphia and worked in a slaughterhouse and began amateur boxing under the watchful eye of old trainer Yank Durham. Frazier went on to have an illustrious amateur record culminating in an Olympic gold medal in 1964. As a professional he quickly destroyed all those who were put in front of him. With Ali banned for political reasons, Frazier won the WBC title by beating Buster Mathis and then unified the belts by overcoming Jimmy Ellis who couldn't continue after the fourth round.

Earlier in his career he was labelled as the 'black Marciano' for his style of releasing nonstop barrages of punches without resting, soon that was changed to 'Smokin' Joe Frazier. The fight of the century finally occurred on 8th March 1971. A classic encounter that will be long remembered between two un-beaten men. Ali danced and threw his laser like punches whilst Joe went hard to the body and kept coming forward. Eventually his signature shot, the left hook, prevailed and dumped Ali to the canvass in the last round. Ali regained com-posure and beat the count, but Frazier was the unanimous winner on points. It was a beautiful fight and the two men's contrasting styles made it one of the most entertaining ever.

After two title defences Frazier came up against an unbeaten George Foreman, who had obliterated into unconsciousness 34 of his last 37 victims. Styles often dictates the outcome of a fight; Frazier could not cope with Fore-man's big long range punches and was knocked down six times before the referee stepped in to end it. Two more contests with Ali were next, the first Frazier lost on points again, the second he couldn't continue into the fifteenth round due to exhaustion. All three of the fights between Frazier and Ali were extremely close. Each's strengths were the other's weakness, their fights were brutal and chess like, taking a toll both physically and mentally on both men.

The only men to beat Joe Frazier were Muhammed Ali and George Foreman, twice each. After retiring Frazier became a trainer to pass on the pearls of the sweet science, one of his pupils being his son Marvin who even had a shot at the title. He sadly passed away in 2011 at the age of 66.

Frazier The Fighter

There are several reasons why Joe Frazier stood out as a unique fighter. Firstly, he was a two-handed body snatcher, who seemed to get stronger as the fight continued and never lost steam. He adopted a catch and kill style by mastering the art of cutting off the ring and forcing his opponents to fight his fight. His left hook was lethal, and he could unleash it with equal ferocity to the body or head. In the examination of Joe Frazier's greatness, we must look at his finest achievement; he won the fight of the century, the biggest most anticipated fight of all time.

"Joe, if you beat this guy, the road the rest of your life will be paved forever no matter what you do. But if he beats you, you'll never get the respect you deserve as heavyweight champion. History will look at you as a caretaker champion who just held the title for him until he got straightened out with the government. And remember, Joe, Clay doesn't want to just beat you. He wants to humiliate you and embarrass you. Beat this guy Joe and they can never take it away from you."
Yank Durham

On Fighting Ali

Ali had never faced a fighter who could get inside him and beat his jab. He was masterful at controlling from a distance and dictating the entire fight at his pace. Frazier forced Ali to fight, hold, and use his legs to try and stay away from danger. Every time Ali tried attacking against Frazier, he found himself on the inside which was Frazier's domain. Once on the inside, Frazier's hands were lightning fast, as was his foot speed. He quickly gained ground and was in Ali's face before he knew it. Frazier used his speed to great effect on Ali. Once on this inside it was impossible to move him off.

Muhammad Ali's jab was his winning tactic that made him great but no fighter succeeded at making Ali miss so many jabs as Joe Frazier did. Frazier's bobbing and weaving skill was the antidote to the Ali Jab. When Frazier made Ali miss with the fastest jab in heavyweight history, he made him pay for it too with massive left hooks to his head and body. Ali always said that Frazier was extremely difficult as hell to hit.

On The Losses To Foreman

The reality is that Frazier was a better fighter than Foreman but couldn't beat him from a style perspective. Adopting his forward pressure style there are two boxers who were made to beat that. George Foreman and Joe Louis.. Frazier, in the same vein as Dempsey, Marciano, and Tyson, could only fight by moving forward and forcing the fight. When Joe came out Smokin, Foreman was like a fire extinguisher. The result would have been the same had Foreman fought Dempsey, Marciano, or Tyson. He would have destroyed them style wise. It is no secret that Mike Tyson wanted nothing to do with fighting Foreman.

Frazier's Style

Joe Frazier was the ultimate catch and kill style fighter. He applied more pressure and no one cut off the ring better than he did. His style was to constantly be in his opponent's chest, wearing them down and applying pressure and punches from every angle available to him.

Because his style required exceptional head movement and timing, it also gave him exceptional defence to go with the offense. He could parry jabs with his right glove, duck under the hooks and right hands and easily counter with a left hook to the head or to the body.

Compared to other infighters, Frazier didn't get hit as much at all. Even when there were no punches coming at him, he constantly bobbed and weaved, his head movement made him extremely elusive. It also allowed him to punch with unpredictability and momentum to add power into those vicious hooks he was famous for. Against a powerful jab he would shuffle his way in, eating up ground and then throw the hooks, he was always slipping and he always hooked off the slip.

Left Hook

Frazier suffered an injury as a child that likely led to the hammer of a left hook he had. He broke his arm in a fall and his family were unable to afford medical treatment or pay for a doctor, so it healed badly, unable to straighten ever again. His signature left hook was born.

'My left arm was seriously damaged because of an ornery three hundred pound hog of ours. Sounds weird, I know, but it's true. This boar hog of ours was so nasty that from time to time I couldn't resist teasing it. Well, one day when I was about eight, I poked it with a stick and ran like hell. Unfortunately, somebody had left the gate to the pigpen open and that damn creature ran straight through, chasing my sorry a**. Scared? Oh yes. I ran like hell and, in my hurry, fell and hit my left arm on a brick.

'The fall tore my arm up bad. But we were too poor to see doctors, so the arm was left to heal on its own. It did, but I was never able to fully straighten it as I was before the accident. The left arm was now crooked, lacking full range of motion. But as it existed, it was as though cocked for the left hook - permanently cocked. Strange for a guy whose success in the world would later depend on what that left could generate.'
Joe Frazier

Joe Frazier was able to knock everyone out with it, if it connected cleanly it was lights out. it was impossible to see the left hook coming, because of his rapid movement, constantly changing levels, bobbing and weaving, feinting and throwing body shots. He would often feint a punch to the head but then went to the body. He would alternate that with changing levels from a half body shot to taking out the head. It was extremely difficult to predict when Frazier was going to throw the left hook. Smokin' Joe did most of his knockouts, with that punch, while he was walking his opponents down.

Joe Frazier could unleash that left hook multiple times. By either hitting the same spot repeatedly or he would target different areas by going to the body and head. This variety left his opponents dazed and confused.

Crab Guard

You would think Frazier would be open for an uppercut bending forward at the waist as much as he did, but he rarely got caught with this punch. This was due to the crab guard that Frazier adopted. This involved holding his guard in a horizontal position with both arms parallel to the floor. With his arms held across his body and face he could slide punches off of by shifting the punches upwards or below.

Inside Fighting

Shorter than a typical heavyweight, Frazier was most dangerous on the inside, taking advantage of his smaller height and arms. Frazier's skill at combination punching on the inside was a nightmare for his opponents, who's height presented a bigger target, and made it impossible to punch with power up close. By applying torque through his shoulders, waist and bending at the hips while throwing his punches, Frazier was able to get his full bodyweight into every punch.

Frazier's combination punches were targeted at the body and head, he headhunted, and body snatched leaving his opponent's no chance to guess what was coming. Frazier was relentless at unloading from all angles. Once on the inside he would use his forearm as a tool. By lifting the horizontal forearm and pressing it against his opponent he could make space for his own punches and restrict them from firing punches back at him.

<u>Head Fighting</u>
Joe Frazier knew head position was critical to balance and disrupted and frustrated his opponents by pushing the tip of his head into their chest or chin. This severely restricted his opponent's ability to throw punches, as they lost their centre and could not get balanced or set to punch, and they were at serious risk of being pushed back and falling over.

Joe Frazier was an incredible fighter, knockout artist and boxer. He is vastly underappreciated and in the shadow of Ali despite winning the biggest fight of all time. He combined attack and defence in one and could mix up punches that were truly explosive and ferocious.

Earnie Shavers – Puncher Of The Century
Record: 74 wins (68 KOs) / 14 Losses
Style: Boxer Puncher/slugger
Signature Technique: Uppercut
Famous KO: Jimmy Ellis KO round 1

"I firmly believe I'm the hardest puncher ever born; people may be able to match me with their best shot for one of mine but everyone of mine has got killer written on it. Only god hits harder than me."
Earnie Shavers

Earnie Shavers was not a world champion but his contribution as one of the (many say 'the') heaviest hitters ever cannot be denied. Because he de didn't win the belt that is not to say he didn't defeat top tier opposition or was a poor boxer. He was around when the heavyweight era was full of class and it just so happened that he had incredible punching power that could trouble them all.

Shavers early record was outstanding, winning 44 of his first 47 fights and a knockout streak of 27, 20 of which were in the first round. He was an early fighter to be managed by controversial character Don King who led him to be a top contender. A brutal KO of Jimmy Ellis in the first round really boosted Shavers onto the world stage. He suffered losses to Jerry Quarry and Bob Stallings and fellow hard hitter Ron Lyle did a number on him in the sixth round. Shavers came back strongly from these losses and dispatched Howard King (another heavy hitter) and then Roy Williams in a savage match that Shavers maintained was the toughest fight in his career.

Known as the "Black Destroyer", Shavers compiled an impressive record, winning 44 of his first 47 fights by knockout; mostly against unremarkable opposition. His KO streak included 27 consecutive knockouts, of which 20 victories were in the first round. He suffered setbacks with losses to Ron Stander and Stan Johnson and an explosive fight with fellow hard hitter Ron Lyle that saw Shavers knocked out in the sixth round.

He began to rise through the ranks of the heavyweight division after he hired a Cleveland-based promoter and ex-con named Don King to be his manager. His wins included a novice Jimmy Young who would later become a top contender. Stepping up the class of opposition, he came to public prominence with a first-round KO of one time WBA heavyweight champion Jimmy Ellis. His progress was halted when he was KO'd in the first round by Jerry Quarry which was followed by another loss to a journeyman Bob Stallings. Shavers then had a thunderous match with hard hitting Ron Lyle but was stopped after six brutal rounds. He then knocked out hard hitter Howard King and beat powerful prospect Roy Williams in a brutal back and forward battle in which Shavers was nearly knocked out. The match Shavers always said was one of the toughest of his whole career.

By the time Shavers fought Muhammad Ali in 1977 he was already 54-5-1, with 52 knockouts. It was a close fight and Ali won on points but had incurred terrible damage from Shavers, including a crushing overhand right in the second round. It was extremely close going into the final round, and it was noted that Ali was on shaky legs. Angelo Dundee in his corner told him "You don't look so good. You better go out and take this round." It was a frantic final round with Ali finishing the strongest at the bell, which is when it often counts the most on the score cards. Many thought Shavers did enough to win the fight and Ali himself said "Shavers was the hardest puncher he ever faced, stating "Earnie hit me so hard, it shook my kinfolk back in Africa".

Shavers went on to have a mixed end to his career, A big first round KO against Ken Norton was notable, especially seeing as Norton had defeated Ali. He fought a tough contest against Larry Holmes trying again for the title, as before it eluded him with Holmes knocking him out in round 11, not though before Shavers had put down Holmes in the seventh in what Holmes said was the hardest punch he ever took in his career. After starting to have retinal eye issues and more losses than wins Shavers eventually retired and hung up his gloves.

Earnie Shavers deserves to be on any list of great punchers but it should also be noted that he would struggle to squeeze into the top ten of all time for one very clear reason, he was not a knockout artist. He was a heavy puncher with tremendous physical power, even Angelo Dundee said: "Earnie wasn't really a good boxer, but God, his power was amazing." Harsh words, and perhaps an exaggeration to call Shavers not a good boxer, he was a good boxer just not a great boxer. He was in an era of great boxers and knock out artists. A knockout artist is not someone who throws wild enormous punches but the fighter who has mastered the sweet science to make it look simple; there is minimalistic cleanness to their punches. Joe Louis and Archie Moore were examples of fighters with the kind of pinpoint accuracy and perfection of technique and mechanics that even to this day remain unsurpassed.

Earnie Shavers was a massive heavy hitter and will be long remembered in the sport of Boxing for his contribution and conduct. We can celebrate his power and destructive ability whilst also recognising the areas that perhaps did not make him as great as others, and understand why he never won the world heavyweight championship.

"Earnie could punch you in the neck with his right hand and break your ankle."
Tex Cobb

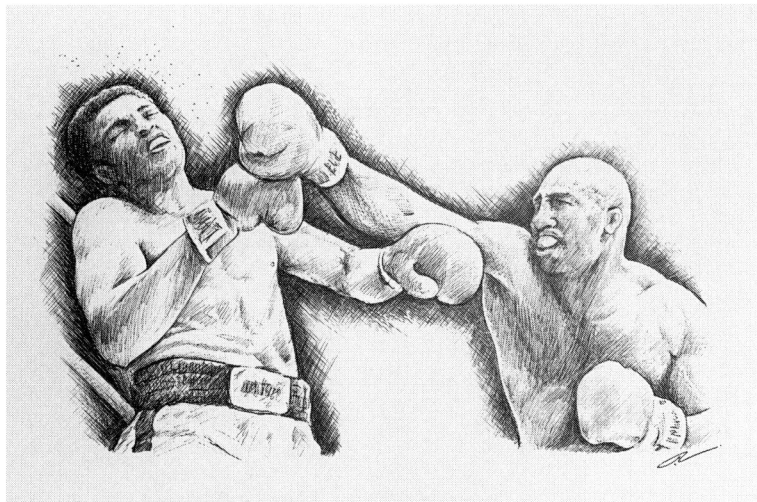

Above: Earnie Shavers

Above: George Foreman

George Foreman – A Tale Of Two Fighters
Record: 81 wins (68 KOs) / 5 Losses
Style: Slugger
Signature Technique: Body Snatching
Famous KO: Round 2 TKO Joe Frazier

"Boxing is like jazz. The better it is, the less people appreciate it."
George Foreman

Arguably the strongest and most dangerous Champ of all time. Foreman was a classic slugger who planted his feet to the ground to produce maximum force into every one of those punches he threw. He is definitely one of the most intimidating and ferocious boxers. He was schooled in the old ways and knew how to smother and trap his opponent's hands to create openings for throwing those big bombs. Against in-fighters he just pushed and bullied them away whilst firing in those dynamite fists.

Like many before him, George Foreman's entry into boxing was a means of escape from the life of early crime he had found himself in. An impressive record as an amateur resulted in a gold medal at the 1968 Olympics at Mexico City in what was incredibly only his 25th fight. Two years after turning professional Foreman was ranked the number one challenger by both the WBA and WBC and had a record of 37-0, 35 by knockout. When Foreman got his shot at the title in 1973, he was the underdog against Smokin Joe Frazier, the first man to beat Muhammed Ali. Foreman utterly destroyed Frazier knocking him down six times before finishing it for good in round 2.

Almost exactly ten years to the day Foreman quit, he returned. 24 fights were won, with 22 by knockout. He fought again for the title at the age of 42 but lost a points decision to Evander Holyfield. Three years later he had another shot against newly crowned champion Michael Moorer. Foreman knocked out Moorer in round 10 becoming the oldest fighter ever to win the heavyweight title and the boxer with the longest time span between winning the title. Nobody had a punch harder than George Foreman a man who captured the heavyweight title twice in his life – 20 years apart, this is an achievement beyond anybody else mentioned in this book, George is special. Not mentioning Foreman's religious transformation that occurred between these events, he was a very different person, but as a boxer he was also totally different. Arguably the George Foreman in his late 40's would have beaten the younger George Foreman.

Foreman's mentor and cornerman, who knocked out more men than anybody else and whose 'ageless' ability helped him hold a light heavyweight title until the age of 48 was – Archie Moor.

The young Foreman was built like an old Victorian toilet with biceps carved out of marble, his physical presence was large and intimidating to other heavyweights and this was a large part of his fight game. Another integral part of his strategy would be to dominate and control the centerline with his strong jolting jab and smashing right hand. He also had skill in neutralizing his opponent's guard, by smothering and disrupting their arms before they could punch. This reduces their ability to produce power and also creates opportunities and openings to unleash punches.

Foreman's punches were all slick and highly dangerous, he had a stiff jab, a horrible right hand, left and right hooks used with his feet and probably the best uppercut in the game. His footwork has been criticized as static and ploddy, I would counter that by saying he knew exactly what he was doing with his feet and was a master of both cutting up the ring and placing his opponent where he wanted them. Which brings us on to the second-generation George Foreman, who had particularly refined this skill and ability.
Before we do though, let us not forget the young George.

First generation George Foreman was a savage and brutal fighter that not only won an Olympic gold medal with less than 2 years boxing experience, but he destroyed two of the all-time great Heavyweight punchers – Joe Frazier and Ken Norton. Sadly, Foreman became more famous during this period for his loss to a returning Muhammed Ali in the infamous rumble in the jungle, which eclipsed many of his own great achievements.

Fast forward 20 years to November the 5th 1994, a 45 year old George Foreman was well into his comeback trail, which had gone extremely well with the exception of point losses to Tommy Morrison and Evander Holyfield. Foreman was to face Michael Moorer the current heavyweight champion with a 35-0 record, a fast and dangerous fighter with slick ring craft who himself had defeated Holyfield. The bout itself had problems in getting officially sanctioned at first as Foreman was viewed as such an outside chance. If you watch, and more importantly listen, to the live commentary from the Foreman-Moorer fight you will hear how (quite rightly) it is pointed out that Moorer was getting well ahead on points, out jabbing Foreman, and by the time the 10th round came about George had lost at least 7 rounds. In his corner, interestingly not only was Archie Moore but also Angelo Dundee who had been in Ali's corner the night of the fateful loss in Zaire. Dundee told Foreman in no uncertain words that going into the 10th round, the only possible way George could win was by a knockout, which is exactly what he did.

Foreman connected with a damaging body shot early in the round which appeared to slow down the normally far more agile Moorer. Foreman began to throw several long wide left hooks that the commentators dismissed as punches of desperation from a losing man. They were not. George knew exactly what he was doing, he had hurt Moorer who was becoming more lethargic and static, no more the elusive moving target he was before. The wide hooks were Foreman placing Moorer exactly where he wanted him and measuring up for a tremendous right hand which inevitably came, broke Moorer's mouthguard, split his lip and sent him to sleep. An act of boxing genius.

The second coming of George Foreman was a more controlled, tactical and patient incarnation. He had not lost any power, if anything he gained more, he was still tremendously strong and spending huge amounts of time in his camp in preparation; working on strength by chopping wood and pulling objects with a harness strapped to his body. He knew how to use his bodyweight and put his hips into every single punch. If there was one punch you did not want to be on the end of it was a George Foreman punch.

"Sure, the fight was fixed, I fixed it with a right hand."
George Foreman

Thomas Hearns
Record: 61 wins (48 KOs) / 5 Losses
Style: Boxer Puncher
Signature Technique: One Two
Famous KO: Jimmy Ellis KO round 4

'Life is one big chance. You know what I'm talking about? Look. You could get mugged, you could get cut or robbed today. So, if you're going to do anything in life, you got to take the chance, man. You got to take it, and if you're fighting, you got to put some hurt on him. I look forward to the, you know, to the combat. It's the chance.'
Thomas Hearns

Thomas Hearns remains one of the most exciting and destructive boxers ever, his fists were loaded with dynamite and he lived by the motto 'destroy or be destroyed'. Growing up in the very rough East side of Detroit, one of nine children he learned early doors to box in the basement of a local church.

Hearns became an outstanding Amateur winning 155 out 163 fights. Incredibly at this point only scoring 11 knockouts. It is a shocking statistic given the professional he was destined to be, and it is also a testament to the man who was to mentor and coach this skinny 6'1 wiry boxer into a world class knockout artist. When they say boxers are born not made, they forgot Emmanuel Steward was churning them out factory style from the Kronk gym. Hearns made his professional debut under Steward at the age of 19 and scored a second round knockout. The next 12 victims he fought never went passed the third round. He was a tornado through the welterweight division and within a year was 28-0 with 26 by KO. The next test for him was mammoth. Pipino Cuevas of Mexico, a man who had reigned as WBA champion since 18 years of age, a knockout artists himself with 24 KO's in wins and 11 title defences. A very dangerous and powerful fighter. The odds were against the skinny tall guy from Detroit, the odds were wrong, Hearns destroyed Cuevas in two rounds, the only knockout defeat in Cuevas' career.

The world began to notice Thomas Hearns, previously labelled the 'Motor City Cobra' due to his height and 78 inch reach, he had earned a new name; 'The Hit Man'. Like a cold mean contract killer he could finish his opponent quickly and move on to the next job. In his words "Fighters I have fought are never the same as they were. I take good care of my people. I can reach deep inside them and cause permanent damage." The next three challengers were all dispatched within the distance and then came the dream boxing fight the world was waiting for. A unification contest between Thomas 'The Hit Man' Hearns and 'Sugar' Ray Leonard. Although the two were acquainted through the Kronk gym, it was somewhat of a grudge match and Hearns was very open about what he had planned to do to Leonard. It was a stunning fight with Hearns the clear leader early on, controlling with his flicker jab and overhand right, Leonard came back strong in the late rounds and the referee stopped the fight in his favour in the fourteenth, to be the first loss suffered by Hearns.

Hearns campaigned back as a light middleweight winning three bouts then challenging Puerto Rico's Wifred Benitez for the WBC title. Hearns won a 15 round decision over a worthy opponent and once again continued his winning ways. The next fight that followed was against the legendary 'Hands of Stone' Roberto Duran of Panama, who is perhaps one of the finest examples of precise and deadly punching ever to be seen. Hearns destroyed Duran within two rounds, finishing the fight with a thundering right hook to the jaw. It was an incredible performance and still seen to this day as one of his best.

Following one more title defence Hearns moved up a weight division again and challenged the undisputed Middleweight Champion of the world 'Marvellous' Marvin Hagler, not exactly an easy first fight at a new weight. This fight later became known as 'The War' and one of the most savage and brutal boxing fights to ever occur. The first round was an incredible display of punching, guts and toughness that you will ever see. This fight could have gone either way with both men continuously unloading on each other, unfortunately for Hearns it was he who fell first in the third round to Hagler's right hand, he beat the count but was not fit to continue. Emmanuel Steward later claimed the first words from Hearns following the Hagler match was 'did the fans enjoy the fight?' It was a battle to be long remembered and epic in all sense of the word.

As usual Hearns came back quickly, he regained his WBC Super Welterweight Title with an 8th round stoppage of Mark Medal and continued to move up three weight classes to capture the WBC Light Heavyweight title with a 10th round stoppage over Dennis Andries. Hearns then went back down to Middleweight to knock out Manuel Roldan for the WBC title and became the first boxer in history to win a world title in four divisions.

A second fight with Sugar Ray Leonard for the WBC Super Middleweight title followed. It was a highly controversial draw with most pundits believing Hearns took victory, even Leonard himself said 'Hearns should have gotten the decision. I admit that.' Hearns continued to win titles including adding the WBA Light Heavyweight Title and WBU and IBO Cruiserweight Titles to his list of accolades. When Hearns finally hung up his gloves at the age of 47 his final professional record was 61-5-1 (48 wins by KO) but his true legacy is as one of greatest fighters and knockout artists of all time.

Hearns was special, very special. He had one of the best one-two's of any fighter in history. With a legendary chopping cross that ended so many careers. Hearns was an incredibly talented and tactical boxer. With the partnership with Emmanuel Steward he was able to turn his lanky frame into a killing machine. To look at Hearns physically as a boxer one would assume he would be a defensive outboxer and use his reach. This was not the case; he was an aggressive and explosive boxer puncher of the finest order. He turned weaknesses to strengths and his strengths became his magic. His lead hand had the versatility to be tailored for any occasion and his devastating right was just vicious.

The Hearns Jab

He utilised one version often called the lazy jab, in which he would delay retracting the hand to block the vision of his opponent. By waiting until the last moment before pulling it back he could hide the incoming cross, he even pinned the opponent's front hand as he stepped in. Hearns could also use a flicker jab and circle to the inside, to control and dictate the pace of the fight by destroying his opponents centre through adopting a superior angle.

The stiff arm jab was used by Hearns to keep his opponent at range and block their vision. He would lean his weight into the opponent's neck, thereby disrupting their balance. He also liked to lower his turn his lead jab and pull the opponent into his punch. This was an intentional move to split, push, or pull away his competitors guard, creating a brief opening for the right cross.

The Hearns Cross

It became known as the chopping right hand and somewhat of a signature of the Kronk style. Unlike a traditional cross the power of his punch wasn't sent forward, but downwards towards to floor. He would pull his hand back and then turn the elbow up at the last moment. This path allowed the punch to crash through the opponent's guard and add incredible velocity and force. It was a tight hammer of a punch incredibly hard to see and defend against.

These one two combinations together with Hearns' hands speed, footwork and ring craft is what made the Hit Man such a great fighter.

Above: Marvin Hagler

Left: Thomas Hearns

Marvin Hagler – The Fighter's Fighter
Record: 62 wins (52 KOs) / 3 losses
Style: Boxer Puncher
Signature Technique: Right Jab
Famous KO: Thomas Hearns KO round 3

'I'm not scared of blood. Matter of fact, it turns me on sometimes. The monster comes out.'
Marvin Hagler

Marvin Hagler had all the traits of a knockout legend. Shaven head, chiselled physique, cold eyes and a stone-cold attitude. His record of destruction and title of undisputed middleweight champion of the world is a legacy that will last forever. Outside the ring, like many, he was a totally different character and devoted to his family, but when the gloves went on he was a killer and no one could stand in his way.

Hagler began to box at 15 years of age and the Petronelli Brothers became his loyal guardians, in his corner during his whole career. He was an outstanding amateur and began boxing five days before his 21st Birthday. He took his time to establish himself in the ranks and after 6 years he challenged for the undisputed world middleweight title and fought a questionable draw with Italian Vito Antuofermo who remained champion. One year later he was the underdog to challenge once again for title. Alan Minter, the champion, had twice beaten Antuofermo so was expected to easily beat Hagler. It was a brutal fight with Hagler opening up Minter's face with vicious punches. The referee was forced to stop the contest in the third round and ugly scenes followed as the British crowd turned on Hagler throwing missiles into the ring. Nevertheless a new enforcer had arrived on the scene, Hagler was now the champion and stepped up his game massively. He was a fighting force and proceeded to beat everyone in the middleweight division who dared to challenge him. He became known as 'Marvellous Marvin Hagler'. Interestingly, years later Minter had commented that upon watching Hagler hit the heavy bag in training it was very different to other fighters, instead of the usual clang of chains heard, there was a screeching noise. It was the result of Hagler corkscrewing and turning his punch into the bag at the last moment. The damage this caused was evident on Minter's face.

"The situation right after the fight wasn't too good; I believe I'm still the only champion in the world who never received the belt inside the ring once you've won the title. I held that against the English fans for a long time but I felt that also motivated me."
Marvin Hagler

When Hagler beat Tony Sibson in 6 rounds, Sibson fought bravely but was hospitalised with 18 stiches around his eyes such was the venom in Haglers punches. Sibson called him 'The Master of Disaster', Alan Minter described him as 'Frightening'.

The Realm Of The Four Kings

And so it began. Over a decade of some of the greatest fights ever and one of the biggest rivalries between four incredible fighters, each carrying a unique and devastating style in their own way. Marvin Hagler, Sugar Ray Leonard, Tommy Hearns and Roberto Duran created a series of encounters in the 1980's that remain today the textbook of technical punching.

Roberto Duran was one of the greatest infighters in history. A tactical genius at close range; precise and lethal, hewas able to come at you from every possible angle. Hagler had an epic battle with Roberto Duran over 15 rounds which he won clearly on points, though he wisely treated Duran with caution and respect.

Going into the fight with Hearns one might expect Hagler to adopt the same cautious strategy. Taking into account Hearn's pedigree and the fact he had the hardest right hand in boxing at that time. It did not quite go like the Duran fight. The fight with Thomas 'The Hitman' Hearns is eight minutes of boxing we are likely to never see the like of again. As we've covered him, Hearns was an incredible fighter who could destroy anyone on any given day with his explosive one two combination and control of the ring. Hearns began the fight as one would expect, at frantic speed and maximum aggression looking to destroy Hagler as quickly as possible. Hagler who normally started slow came out like a man possessed with ferocity and destruction and absolutely battered Hearns. The resulting fight was an incredible lesson in punching from both sides. Three minutes of absolute mayhem and madness, each fighter being rocked by the other. At the bell at the end of the first round Hagler was cut and Hearns unsteady. In the second round the onslaught continued from both sides though Hearns was beginning to look shakier and more desperate. Twice during the round the referee halted proceedings to have the ringside doctor check Haglers cuts. Desperation and the need to finish proceedings from both sides was pressing. The clock was ticking on Hearns' legs and Hagler's cuts. Hagler leaped across the ring and threw a left and right that spun Hearns around, two more power rights and he was done and flat on his back. Hearns managed to get up at the count of 9 but the glassy eyes and wobbly legs put him in no shape to continue. An absolute master class in fighting by Marvin Hagler.

Sugar Ray Leonard was a completely different proposition to both Duran and Hearns. Crafty and elusive, Leonard had an exceptional talent for controlling the ring. Leonard was not just a boxer with nice footwork; he had a killer instinct when needed and could also knock people out, he was not without power. To defeat Hagler he would need to use all of his masterful footwork, timing, speed and reflexes and produce the greatest performance of his life. Hagler would need to do what he did against Hearns and Duran and dominate the fight. With Hearns it was over early and with Duran it went the distance, but the result was the same. One issue with the Leonard fight was Hagler was starting to get passed his prime, father time was catching up. They say when a fighter gets older the first thing to go is his speed, this was evident during the Leonard fight. Both Hagler's hand speed and mobility were not as sharp as when he fought Hearns. The outcome of the fight was a points win to Leonard though it was a highly controversial fight as many felt (including Marvin) that he did enough to win it. Some of the judges' score cards are 'off' for sure, either way you look at it is was extremely close and the result takes nothing away from the legacy of Marvin Hagler. As usual for him, Hagler started the fight slower feeling his way in, Leonard used his footwork well and refused to engage in a slug fest like Hearns had. Hagler also made a strange tactical decision to use his orthodox stance much more than normal in the early rounds of this fight. In the later rounds it was evident Hagler was much stronger, never stepping back and always pressing forward. He was far more overwhelming and hitting Leonard with more frequency with both his jab and longer combinations. Leonard was under considerable pressure but from the judges position it seemed all too late and the decision went to Leonard.

"Even though the outcome wasn't the way it should have been, publicly I still feel in my heart I won the Sugar Ray Leonard fight."
Marvin Hagler

Style

Hagler's style was different, very different. His was as a right-handed southpaw. Boxers usually lead with their weak hand, allowing for an increase in power driven through the body from the feet up into the stronger back hand, which often delivers the knockout punch. Hagler switched constantly from southpaw to orthodox, with equal power in both hands, his transitions were effortless and perfect. He could attack and damage both the body and head, creating havoc and confusion in his opponents. He would often start a fight on the outside, control from there and then move inside going for the kill.

Working on the outside Hagler would control the fight and wear down the opponent with long range attacks to open their guard up. Once that happened he was quickly in. Once on the inside Hagler perfected the placement of his head between the shoulder and neck of his opponent. This severely disrupted their balance and compromised their centre of gravity. It also forced their head up open for attacks. Hagler frequently knocked opponents out at close range by putting his full force and body weight into each and every punch through the stance switches, he caused terrible problems for anyone once there.

Lead Hand

Being a right-handed southpaw also meant his frequent and thunderous jab was with his strongest lead hand. Hagler's jab could itself cause considerable damage, not only a setup but as a standalone punch.

Hagler's lead hand was a unique blend of techniques with various manifestations of power. Most frightening of all was his 'Gazelle' punch. This punch involved Hagler covering massive distance across the ring in a shuffle, or sometimes a jump, with all of his body weight being pushed through into the right leg. He added full body rotation and twist to produce a huge amount of devastating force into his fist. The gazelle punch has been used by other fighters before, such as Joe Frazier, usually the punch would appear as a hook but Hagler's was different. He adopted a line more akin to a jab, this made it extremely difficult to see and defend against. The angle of the punch was extremely tight and the power was horrific.

Another trademark of Marvin Hagler's style was constant head movement across his centreline. Along with being an elusive moving target that was hard to hit he was also loading kinetic energy into his lower body with every slip, this was channelled into his persistent multi-angle punches.

Following the disputed loss to Leonard, Hagler departed the ring that night in absolute disgust and never fought again. He permanently retired and moved to Italy and whilst being devoted to his family also embarked on a movie career.

The passing of Marvin Hagler in 2021 to sudden illness was a huge loss to the boxing world. He retired with a record of sixty-two wins, three losses and three draws. Marvin Hagler is one of the most underrated boxers of the last century, in many ways he was the perfect boxer. Aggression and force forged with intelligence and strategy; he owned the middleweight division. All this made him a devastatingly powerful puncher and one of the greatest boxers who ever lived.

'He had heavy hands and was very strong. He could knock you out with either hand. He had the balls, the heart, and the mind to win. He was ambidextrous. I consider Marvin one of the best that I fought. And I fought in the golden era of boxing.'
Sugar Ray Leonard

'I hit him with everything but the kitchen sink. He continued and kept coming forward. I moved him but he just kept coming forward.'
Thomas Hearns

"The only difference between street fighting and boxing is there's a ref there stopping me from killing you"
Marvin Hagler

Roberto Duran – Hands of Stone
Record: 103 wins (70 KOs) / 16 Losses
Style: In fighter
Signature Technique: Jab
Famous KO: Davey Moore Round 8

"I am not an animal in my personal life," Duran said. "But in the ring there is
an animal inside me. Sometimes it roars when the first bell rings. Sometimes it
springs out later in a fight. But I can always feel it there, driving me and pushing
me forward. It is what makes me win. It makes me enjoy fighting."
Roberto Duran

Roberto Duran was the epitome of what a knockout artist boxer should
be. Hard as nails, he was mean, tough and angry, and that was before he
stepped in the ring. Inside the ring he was dog fighting for his life, the fire in his
belly ignited from a poor childhood sparked the aggression and beast within.

Duran grew up fighting on the dangerous streets of Panama. Son of
a Mexican father and Panamanian mother, fighting was something he was well
accustomed to in his childhood and teen years.

Turning professional at sixteen, his first run at boxing was far from
successful, losing four contests. However, he soon settled into his role and an
unbeaten run of over fifty contests saw him dominate the lightweight divisions
before he challenged at three higher weights. With a list of world title fights
as long as your arm, he began in 1972 against classy WBA Champion Ken
Buchanan of Scotland. Buchanan was stopped in the thirteenth round from what
he claimed was a low blow, when you entered the ring with Duran you were
pretty much in a street fight.

Over the next six years Duran dominated the lightweight division
knocking out all who challenged him. He typically fought two fights per year
before he unified the division by knocking out his old nemesis WBC Champion
Esteban De Jesus. Next it was time for the welterweights. In June 1980 nobody
gave Roberto Duran half a chance against the talented and charismatic Sugar
Ray Leonard. It was a classic encounter of two contrasting styles, Leonard
dancing and boxing, Duran pressing and fighting. In a result that nobody expected, Duran won on points. It was his biggest victory, won through relentless
attacking and determination. Six months later there was an inexplicable turn of
events in the rematch. Leonard was on phenomenal form picking away at Duran
and using his biggest asset, his footwork, to great advantage. In the eighth
round, Duran turned his back and refused to continue in what became known as
the 'no mas' no more fight. It is still talked about to this day, Duran had looked fit
and strong though was being well out boxed on this occasion. It was a humiliation, particularly in his homeland of Panama where the macho culture prevails.

In an effort to redeem his pride Duran stepped up to the light medals, first challenging WBC Champion Wilfred Benitez, this resulted in an unsuccessful points draw. An eighth-round knockout of WBA Champion Davey Moore, however, delivered another belt. Now it was time to challenge the second of the four kings, Marvelous Marvin Hagler. Most thought Duran had bitten of more than he could chew taking this fight. It was an incredible performance going the full distance (the first time ever for Hagler), Duran bravely scrapped his way through but lost on points.

The final king to challenge was Thomas 'The Hit Man' Hearns for the WBC light middleweight title. Hearns was on stunning form and as a boxer puncher against an infighter, Duran had as much chance as Joe Frazier against George Foreman. It was a lesson in jab and cross with Hearns doing to Duran what Hagler had done to Hearns. The right hand that knocked out Duran was possibly one of the finest punches caught on camera ever. By rights Duran should have retired and called it a day on a great career. Not likely. He outpointed Iran Barkley to add another middleweight title.

Barkley was considerably heavier and stronger and had beaten Thomas Hearns who had previously given Duran such a hiding. Duran was in his element, boxing beautifully and tearing up Barkley with hooks and crosses, putting him down in the 11th.

The Barkley fight was his last truly great performance before continuing for another decade well past his best years. Even during this period, well into his forties, he was still troubling every top fighter. His legendary status still well intact.

When one examines the career of Roberto Duran it really needs to be taken in its entirety. Unbeatable for 13 years with a peak record of 72-1 and 56 knockouts, undefeated as world lightweight champion for 6 years and he also won the world welterweight title. Champion across four divisions - lightweight (1972-79), welterweight (1980), junior middleweight (1983) and middleweight (1989-90). As the King of the lightweights he successfully defended the title 12 times, 11 by knockout. In his career he stopped 21 opponents in the first round, 31 within the first 3 rounds. He fought until the age of 50 with a final career record of 103-16 (70 KOs). Roberto Duran never avoided another man in his life, if he could have dug up and revived champions of the past, he would have had a crack. The man was a legend.

In looking at Roberto Duran's style it is worth recognising that like many great fighters and knockout artists he evolved and developed over time to reach a peak. With a starting point of natural talent, aggression and strength this began as a ferocious, street fighting, slugging onslaught with murderous intent. He had power in his fists, could work the body and deck a man with his right hand.

Old timer trainer Ray Arcel was enlisted to take all of Duran's natural attributes, upgrade him and make him into the complete fighter. He succeeded, Duran became an infighter and a boxer puncher.

Angelo Dundee said of Duran "One gets the impression of Duran is that he's a tough, rough brawler who just wades in and ducks nothing. But all you have to do is look at his face to see that is nonsense. He's not marked up. He does a lot of cute things in there."

Although it's true that he rarely took a step back ,Duran also developed a good defence. Excellent head movement off the centreline, angles from slips to launch powerful counter attacks, he knew how to load his body up and turn a defensive move into a vicious counterattack. He knew how to feint and parry, to create openings and opportunities. His defensive moves had attacking intent. Carlos Palomino, who lost a 10 round decision to Duran stated "He's good inside, very good, strong physically. The one thing that surprised me the most was his quickness. And his defensive ability. He moves his head a lot, feints a lot. He's not an easy man to hit."

When it comes down to infighting it can be truly said that Duran had mastered and refined this art. He could knock a man out from a very short distance. Thanks to Ray Arcel he was also extremely skilful and dangerous on the outside. He could control the distance and dictate effortless changes between inside and outside, to cause all sorts of problems to any opponent.

Typically, Duran would use jabs, slips and feints to smash his way inside, he was very good at trapping his opponents guard and getting underneath. Once he had this control it was like the other man was caught in a spider's web. One hand could hit whilst the other pinned and created the opening, it severely disturbed the opponent's balance and centre of gravity. In this position Duran would unleash multiple hooks at close range, each one causing maximum damage, if the first didn't cause a knockout, the second third or fourth would.

Duran was also a master of finding incredibly tight angles, sandwiching himself into his opponent, carrying his own arms tight to his body. From here he could exert control, beat the opponent to the punch and evade any counterattack with ease. He had great sensitivity sensing and feeling his opponent's movements and weight distribution, they were literally trapped with nowhere to go. Pushing his head into his opponent shoulder and creating a diagonal line from head to hips gave him space to operate and go to work. The leverage and power he could produce from this position was extraordinary.

"Duran knew how to fight. He knew what to do. If he looked at the corner the only thing I ever had to do was pretend to jab, once he was using his jab I knew he'd have no trouble. Even more important he knew how to think. When you talk about great fighters, always remember there was a guy named Roberto Duran. He was never given the opportunity to really display his wares because at his peak, he was overshadowed by Muhammad Ali."
Ray Arcel

Above: *Roberto Duran*

Above: *Mike Tyson*

Mike Tyson – A blast from the past
Record: 50 wins (44 KOs) / 6 Losses
Style: In fighter
Signature Technique: Double upper cut body and face
Famous KO: Michael Spinks Round 1

"I'm the best ever. I'm the most brutal and vicious, and most ruthless champion there's ever been. There's no one can stop me. Lennox is a conqueror? No, I'm Alexander, he's no Alexander. I'm the best ever! There's never been anybody as ruthless! I'm Sonny Liston, I'm Jack Dempsey. There's no one like me. I'm from their cloth. There's no one that can match me. My style is impetuous, my defence is impregnable, and I'm just ferocious."
Mike Tyson

Mike Tyson was the master of putting pressure on his opponents. Rapid head movement with a disciplined guard and blitzing hand speed made him both dangerous and elusive to catch. Being only 5'10 in a division of giants became his advantage enabling him to generate power using upward force.

Tyson became the youngest heavyweight champion of the world in 1988 at the age of 20. He was the protégé and adopted son of legendary trainer Cus D'Amato who trained Tyson from the age of 12. On very rare occasions in the boxing world a partnership will occur that will set to ignite something truly special, this was one of those partnerships. D'Amato was approaching retirement and old age. He had a pedigree for training champions along with being a boxing historian and student of the sweet science. Tyson was a juvenile delinquent full of aggression and anger, after being arrested 38 times he had spent most of his childhood in detention centers. With average height and a very heavy, naturally muscular, physique. The two worked together and developed a unique style of boxing and body mechanics that has yet to be even slightly emulated or copied. The methodology and techniques are classic old school boxing. The style played to Tyson's natural attributes and made him truly ferocious and unstoppable when he was at his physical peak.

D'Amato put Tyson through a punishing training regimen, which involved him training every day after school. Tyson had a string of successful amateur fights and also "smokers" which were unsanctioned matches against older opponents. He failed to make the 1984 Olympic team after losing to future gold medallist Tillman. So D'Amato quickly entered Tyson into the professional ranks at the age of eighteen having his first fight on 6th March 1985 for the sum of $500. The opponent, Hector Mercedes, was knocked out in the first round, Tyson quickly followed that up with a string of early round knockouts.

Tyson was even shorter than Marciano and came weaving in from a crouch with upward rapid punches, superb head movement, balance and explosive power. The nickname "Iron Mike" was soon given to the youngster who intimidated his opponents – they rarely made it past the first round or two. Unfortunately, after only eight months of Tyson's professional career, D'Amato passed away.

By 1986 Tyson's record was 22-0, 21 by KO. The World Heavyweight Championship was, at that time, in a poor state (not too far off from today!), Larry Holmes had lost his title to Michael Spinks who held one belt, Trevor Berbick and Tim Witherspoon held others. There were also half a dozen others claiming different titles. Don King, the promoter who controlled heavyweight boxing, began organising a series of bouts to eventually lead to one undisputed Champion.

Tyson's reign began on 22 November when he challenged Trevor Berbick for the WBC belt. Unlike those that had fallen before him, Berbick refused to be intimidated and came out fighting. For little good it did him, in the second round a succession of left hooks smashed Berbick who was on the canvass twice, he rose but his legs were gone. The referee who stopped the fight, later said 'Everything he'd got had "good night" written all over it'. At the age of 20 years Tyson had surpassed Floyd Patterson's record to become the youngest heavyweight champion in history.

On August 1, 1990 Tyson had become the first heavyweight to own all three major boxing belts after taking the WBA title from James Smith and the International Boxing Federation title from Tony Tucker. Other notable defences came against Frank Bruno who was knocked out in the fifth round and Carl Williams who went down in the first. Everything came to a crushing end on February 11th 1990 with one of the greatest boxing upsets of all time. It was clearly an 'off' night for Tyson who was beginning to dominate headlines with his social and private life, which seemed in turmoil. Not to take anything away from Buster Douglas, who put up a fantastic performance and survived an eighth round knock down to come back and knock out Tyson in the tenth round. It was a stunning upset.

The following year in 1991 Tyson was jailed for three years on rape charges and did not box again until 1995. After several early round knockouts of low-level opposition he was set to face Evander Holyfield for the heavyweight title. Holyfield had knocked out Douglas and was the new and undisputed Heavyweight Champion of the world.

The night of November 9, 1996 was unsuccessful for Tyson, despite his claims of illegal headbutts, Holyfield knocked out Tyson in the eleventh round becoming the second person to win a heavyweight championship belt three times. A massively hyped rematch on June 28, 1997, saw the two boxers facing off yet again. The fight set a record for being both the most pay per views in history (over 2 million) and the then highest paid purse to boxers. It will also forever go down in history as 'that fight'.

In the third round Tyson grabbed Holyfield and bit both of his ears, completely severing a piece of the right ear. Despite Tyson claiming this was retaliation for Holyfield's illegal head butts from their previous match he was immediately disqualified. And things just went from bad to worse.

The Nevada State Athletic Commission revoked Tyson's boxing license and fined the boxer $3 million for biting Holyfield. Next, he was fighting again in 2002 for the WBC, IBF and IBO belts against Lennox Lewis. Tyson was in decline and not at all the same fighter he once was. Losing by knockout he went to lose more fights than he won and retired in 2005. In a total of 58 fights in his professional career, Tyson had won 50 with 44 of them being by knockout.

Mike Tyson had a railroad of a career, he was a different fighter after the three years in prison and he lost everything, including the people that had supported him in his early career. The Mike Tyson of the late 1980's was one of the most ferocious and technically brilliant KO artists ever to walk the earth. He will long be remembered in history as a great boxer with many believing that he would have destroyed both Holyfield and Lewis in his prime under Cus D'Amato.

Let us examine some of the unique aspects of Tyson's style:

Stance:

Tyson was very short for a heavyweight and often giving away more than 6 inches of height to his opponent., He exaggerated this position even more by fighting from a very low crouch. Along with making him more elusive to hit, this position lowered his center of gravity enabling him to produce more power from the ground into his powerful legs and hips, which made his power incredible.

Tyson did not fight side on like most boxers do, he was at least 45 degrees forward, often square when he came inside. This allowed him to control the ring and bully his opponent with both hands. Yes, he was a larger target to hit but he overcame this and created an advantage through his footwork.

Footwork:

Tyson was never static; his method was high octane with short fast sliding and skipping steps at a variety of angles (often changing stance). He would cut off the ring quickly and the terrified opponent would find themselves trapped into a corner being pulverized from every angle. His movements are what we call 'active defensive' because he was elusive, unpredictable and hard to hit but it was also extremely aggressive and offensive. This method of frantic explosive movement is very much akin to 'fight like your clothes are on fire'. One needs a high degree of physical conditioning and aggressive intent to do this.

Speed:

For a heavyweight Tyson had incredible speed, he understood that although lacking the mass and weight of his opponents he could generate power with lightning speed and clever mechanics. Continuous rapid-fire hitting does not give your opponent a chance to think let alone set up a defense. Always focus on speed and quickness in training, slow and heavy punches are like cannonballs compared to the fast bullets of a machine gun-like quick light punch. The key is the strength and structure and the base from which the bullet is fired.

Broken Rhythm:

Most fighters move and attack to a set rhythm, they match each other in speed and timing and look for a gap or mistake within that rhythm to take advantage. Tyson refused to match or even acknowledge his opponent's rhythm and they could barely catch breath to keep up to his. This style interrupts the most composed fighter, Tyson was like a ball of fire in the ring, an incredible energy that will overcome and consume anything that stands in its way.

Body Snatching:

Tyson would relentlessly attack the body with venomous punches, this is a rare ability and skill in modern boxing where it is more common to chase the head. The old school boxers knew that to damage a man's abdomen would be like destroying the engine of a car, it would render the vehicle immobile. In a difficult confrontation with a defensive fighter who is protective of their head, devastating body snatching can destroy both his frame and will.

Angles:

Cus D'Amato famously said that the sweet science of boxing was being able to hit in a position where the opponent could not hit. His student Tyson had a mastery of angles enabling him to hit from a huge variety of unorthodox positions. He would never attack straight on but laterally side to side, zig zagging like a crab from his low crouch and hitting with lightning speed and ferocious power.

Pivot shifting:

Tyson would shift effortlessly between orthodox and southpaw, hitting in both stances. This is a rare skill in a heavyweight (mastered by Bob Fitzsimmons 100 years earlier), this enabled him to be both elusive, hitting from a variety of angles, and to get maximum power and leverage into all his punches by being able to fully twist and torque his hips.

Head Movement:

A significant part of Tyson's style was his quick almost psychic head movement to evade attacks, he would often slip a punch whilst actually countering and hitting on the slip. His speed and awareness at doing this was incredible. He was extremely disciplined with his guard, holding his hands high up to his temple as a second line of defense, this is where the name 'peek a boo' originates.

Conditioning:

Tyson had a phenomenal work ethic when it came to his fitness, he would wake at 4am and undertake a long run knowing his opponent would still be asleep. Along with multiple rounds of sparring, pad work, bag work and skipping he engaged in a huge volume of daily calisthenics – sit ups, push-ups, neck rolls etc. Hundreds to thousands of each exercise, he preferred this approach over weight training as he felt it kept his speed and his ability to relax his muscles.

Mentality:

Cus D'Amato spent as much time training Tyson on the art of psychological warfare as ring craft. He installed a frightening mentality that began with him not hitting his opponents but punching straight through them. He asked him to imagine breaking ribs, exploding livers and even pushing his opponents nose into their brain. Tyson was already full of rage but D'Amato taught him how to really damage a person.

History:

Mike Tyson became a boxing historian alongside D'Amato. They studied hard; reading and watching old manuals and footage from days gone by of all the boxing greats. Tyson loved the old fighters like Dempsey and Marciano and copied key elements of their styles, their techniques and their body mechanics. He became a student of the science and looked to the past for key lessons.

Learning The Tyson Style

The stance is a deep crouch and should not be square until the opportunity presents, a 45-degree angle is ideal. The guard must be held higher than normal, fists at the side of the temple, chin tucked in and shoulders raised. Work in and out by bobbing and weaving, in this style you need to be continuously moving and changing hence the demand for a very high level of physical fitness. Being static does not work in this style. You need to move laterally in zig zag directions when you throw every punch, moving the head will move the body.

Weapons of choice are the left hook and slipping off the opponents jab with right hooks to the ribs and swinging to the left with left liver shots. Once in close the uppercut and short overhand right can come into play. Body snatch to make the opponent drop their guard then attack the head.

In this method you are on the front foot carrying the fight to the opponent, you need a high level of both fitness and aggression.

Mastering The Art Of In Fighting

A boxer of Tyson's short, stocky and muscular build was almost made to fight on the inside, he would have been severely handicapped against tall long-range fighters, so needed to make his way in as quickly as possible and get to work. Once a skilled in-fighter is in their preferred range it is extremely difficult to get them out.

As mentioned, Tyson was extremely disciplined with his fighting guard, his arms almost glued to his head as a secondary line of defence if all the head movement didn't work. Once inside, the body snatching occurred that will wear down and break a fighter's spirit. These rapid body hits tire and drain the opponent without their realisation until it's too late.

To effectively in-fight you need to get in and then learn to twist and torque full power and put body weight into each short blow as there is not much room for leverage, and then get back out.

Slipping

Although it seems a defensive move the mentality of Tyson's rapid left and right slipping was not just to avoid punches but to work in through various angles where he could hit freely with both hands without being hit. It was a countering technique. The movement should be small just enough to evade the punch if it lightly grazes the guard that is perfect. A slip with a side step and shift of weight is the perfect position to launch a devastating body blow.

Mike Tyson Combinations

Tyson was a natural body snatcher as is often the way for shorter fighters who adopt a deep crouching stance. His punch combinations would often begin with or end with a body blow, typically the hook or uppercut. This strategy would wear down opponents, punish and bully them and of course tempt them to drop their guard, creating an opening to the head.

The 4 main types of body punches Tyson used were:
- Left Jab
- Right Cross
- Hook
- Uppercut

Being in a 45-degree stance (more square when he was very close) enabled him to throw combinations (punches in bunches he called them) from both sides and mix them up. This would also maximise his use of angles, take his head off the centre line and confuse his opponent with the broken and unorthodox rhythm. He would generally close the gap with a long-range punch like a jab as he slipped, weaved and stepped in to his opponent at frantic pace. He was a master of cutting off the ring, which is trapping your opponent with no space to move and escape, such as in the corner. To do this he would often use his jab, body jabs, gazelle (leaping) left hooks and straight rights as he zig zagged in towards his prey.

Once he was in range, Tyson would be in his element to body snatch with a huge variety of combinations, some of his favourites included:

- Left hook to the body, left uppercut
- Right uppercut, right hook to the body
- Left body hook, right head hook
- Right body hook left uppercut
- Continuous left hooks to the body

How To Overcome The Tyson Style

Tyson was not undefeated; he came unstuck in his later career several times and each time it was generally against a taller boxer who learned how to keep him away and use the jab effectively. Unfortunately though, we still do not get an accurate picture of this being the correct method because none of his defeats occurred in his prime.

At his peak, Tyson was consistently knocking out larger more experienced boxers. There are two eras of Mike Tyson and in the latter era he was a very different boxer who was mentally completely different with a style that was much more static and less explosive, with both his fitness and aggression severely diminished.

To find the answer on how to meet his style effectively we need to go much further back; to the great Jack Dempsey who came unstuck in his prime to Gene Tunney in the largest purse ever fought for in 1926. Dempsey was a fighter of the Tyson style (Tyson actually adored and emulated Dempsey), a deep croucher who was incredibly aggressive throwing hooks, swings and shots from every possible angle with his head swinging like a tree in a hurricane.

Tunney beat Dempsey not by using a jab but by using footwork. He used quick footwork to lean back on Dempsey's dangerous swings. From here he launched sharp and hard straight left and right punches in return. He was an incredible defensive counter puncher and utilised this with his superior balance and footwork. He also prepared well in advance by adjusting his punching to hit low into Dempsey's head, which was often at waist height. Also, he did use his jab to great effect, no croucher can stay down forever and the moment Dempsey came up he would be hit by a masterful straight left. Tunney beat Dempsey with IQ, he had an amazing boxing brain and could study his opponent and work out the right strategy, fighting for him was like a game of chess. Dempsey gets the glory as the most exciting and explosive fighter but it is no surprise that Tunney has an almost perfect record of 88 wins, never knocked out and only one loss on points, which he subsequently avenged.

Roy Jones Jnr
Record: 66 wins (47 KOs) / 9 Losses
Style: Boxer Puncher
Signature Technique: Lead hand diving punch
Famous KO: Jorge Vaca Round 2

'When I was a kid, I had a desire to fight and I couldn't understand what it was. I used to fight, I used to wanna fight, but I wouldn't fight just for the fun of it. What I would do was, even in Elementary school, if I saw a bigger kid pick on a smaller kid - that was my chance. So, when I used to go to school, I was the police – because if I caught you picking on somebody we're gonna fight because that's what I'd been waiting for.'
Roy Jones Jr.

Roy Jones Jr is an incredibly talented and creative boxer with real knock out ability. Jones was named fighter of the decade in the 1990's, he was the first person to win heavyweight and middleweight world title. He has also held WBC, IBO, IBA and WBF titles, a record seven belts at one time. Jones was renowned for his blistering speed, technical boxing, power and razor-sharp reflexes.

Roy Jones Sr was a Vietnam War Veteran who was awarded the bronze star for valor, he introduced his son to boxing and forced him to endure a brutal early training program that almost broke him. He would regularly beat him with objects and subject him to mental abuse, he even shot his dog dead to teach him a lesson.

'After a while I didn't care about getting hurt or dying anymore. I was in pain all day, every day, I was so scared of my father. He'd pull up in his truck and start looking for something I'd done wrong. There was no escape, no excuse, no way out of nothing. .. Getting hurt or dying might've been better than the life I was living. I used to think about killin' myself anyway.'
Roy Jones Jr

Jones Sr managed Jones Jr throughout his amateur boxing years and the first couple of years of his professional career. The relationship came to a head in 1992 when Jones Jr had enough of the bullying, fired his father and replaced him with Alton Merkerson.

Jones came into the public eye during the Seoul 1988 Olympic Games when he was robbed of a gold medal in one of the worst judging fiascos in history. He had not dropped a round in the games and battered his Korean opponent Park Si-Hun over 3 rounds. The judges were later suspended but the result was never put right.

The professional career of Jones started with a bang with his first

fifteen wins by KO. He then faced former champ Jorge Vaca in what was intended to be a bigger test and Jones knocked him out within the first round.
Within five years he was fighting for the title against undefeated IBF super middleweight James Toney. It was a massively hyped fight and Jones was by far the superior boxer, decking Toney in round three then going on to take the decision unanimously on points.

In the following 12 months Jones destroyed anyone put in front of him, mostly by KO, including former lightweight champion Vinny Pazienza in round six. Ridiculously, he participated in two paid sporting events in one day. A basketball game and a title fight against a future world champion Eric Lucas who was knocked out in round eleven.

Soon, Roy Jones was one of the elite champions holding titles in three weight divisions, the titles and belts kept coming with the occasional loss which he mostly avenged. He won the WBA Heavyweight title against John Ruiz who had defeated Evander Holyfield, it was the first time in over 100 years that a former middleweight champion had held the Heavyweight crown. Jones topped that off by going back down to light heavyweight and defeated Antonio Tarver to regain that belt, an achievement only done once before, by the great Bob Fitzsimmons.

Unfortunately, the rematch and next few years of fighting went less successfully for Jones as age crept up and losses too. There were some big wins in that period too, including a late surge of wins at cruiserweight capturing both the WBF and WBU titles before finally announcing his retirement.

In breaking down the style of Roy Jones Jr it must first be understood that he is possibly the most gifted fighter to ever enter the ring. His combination of power, hand speed, complex and unorthodox footwork was leagues above anyone when in his prime. He could do the things that Muhammed Ali and Sugar Ray Leonard did but he could also do the things that Joe Frazier and George Foreman did too. At his best he was capable of doing anything he wanted. Withequal power in both hands, he threw them from all angles, both stances and sometimes.....from behind his back! He would be frantically fast in a continuous blur of motion and then somehow completely freeze, as if somehow stopping time, and completely disrupt his opponent.

The Roy Jones Jr style is not one for the textbook or something to imitate. He had a gift from god, like Maradona in football. He broke all the rules of boxing and created something else, something that went beyond our understanding of the art.

A favoured technique of his was a high-risk punch launched whilst charging forward with arms wide open and chin sticking out. The level of danger and threat to himself is not only from the over-commitment and exposed chin, but also the inability to defend anything coming in. He was never knocked out doing this and in fact to the contrary knocked out several opponents.

By utilising his lead right hand as his main tool (the opposite way around to most fighters), his rear hand would be used to control distance, accuracy and set up combinations, like a jab is normally used. Of course, it had knock out power too though. Jones's cross was an entry technique which he used to come in and fire off a combo, pivot and leave by different route. He would commonly switch step into an open, or southpaw stance and then manoeuvre out from either side.

Pivoting off the lead foot and switching stances is a favoured technique of in fighters like Joe Frazier, Dempsey and Tyson. The only difference being they would stay inside and go toe-to-toe, always pressing forward. Jones would alternate between long and short range. This made him very difficult to hit and it very difficult to predict where his next punch or combination was coming from.

The lead right hand contained tremendous power and venom. Opponents would be dazed and confused about which hand was coming. It's almost like he had the ability to talk backwards but in physical terms. Often the punches would start from the waist and travel in loops. Alongside not knowing which way he was coming it was impossible to predict a hook, uppercut, jab or a cross.

There will never be another Roy Jones Jr, he was truly a one of a kind and a stunning, creative and unpredictable knockout artist.

Roy Jones Jnr Honours Include:

- 1986 Goodwill Games Silver Medal
- 1986 Golden Gloves Champion
- 1987 National Golden Gloves Champion
- 1988 Olympic Games Silver Medal
- WBC International Americas Super Middleweight Title
- IBF Middleweight Title
- IBF Super Middleweight Title
- WBO NABO Light Heavyweight Title
- WBC Interim Light Heavyweight Title
- IBC Light Heavyweight Title
- WBC Light Heavyweight Title
- WBA Light Heavyweight Title
- IBF Light Heavyweight Title
- IBO Light Heavyweight Title
- WBF Light Heavyweight Title
- IBA Light Heavyweight Title
- Ring Magazine Light Heavyweight Title
- UBO Intercontinental Cruiserweight Title
- WBU (German Version) Cruiserweight Title
- WBF Cruiserweight Title
- WBA Heavyweight Title
- Ring Magazine Fighter of the Year 1994

- World Boxing Hall of Fame Fighter of the Year 2003
- Best Boxer ESPY Award x3 (1996, 2000, 2003)
- Boxing Writers Association of America Fighter of the Decade - 1990's
- Most Wins in Unified Light Heavyweight Title Bouts in History (12)

Above: Roy Jones Jr

Above: Deontay Wilder

Deontay Wilder – The Bronze Bomber
Record: 42 wins (41 KOs) / 1 Loss
Style: Boxer Puncher
Signature Technique: Right Cross
Famous KO: Dominic Breazeale KO round 1

"God definitely blessed me with power. I still don't know the limits of my own power."
Deontay Wilder

Wilder is a powerhouse of a heavyweight fighter who had a rapid rise to glory after turning to boxing to financially support his daughter who was born with spina bifida. A talented athlete playing college level Basketball and Football, he was forced to quit studies and instead work two jobs. Boxing offered him an olive branch and he grabbed it in both hands.

Following a short amateur career, which culminated in winning the U.S. Olympic trials and a bronze medal at the 2008 Beijing Olympic Games, he turned professional. The first 32 of his professional contests were all won by knockout, usually within 5 rounds and more than half in the first round. He quickly enlisted trainer Mark Breland, himself a former world champion and Olympic gold medal winner. Wilder had tremendous natural power and a mammoth 84-inch reach, Breland was able to add some sweet science to the potent mix.

He landed a shot at the Heavyweight title in 2015 against Bermane Stiverne. Although the undisputed winner, it was the first time he went the distance and had to work for the title despite knocking Stiverne down in the second and seventh rounds.

Wilder had a string of successful title defences, proving his own toughness and durability in the fourth of them to Chris Arreola when he broke his right hand in the fourth round and tore his bicep. He fought on one-handed stopping Arreola in the eighth round.

Following surgery on both injuries, Wilder made it abundantly clear his goal was to unify the heavyweight division and take on anyone he could. A rematch beckoned with Bermane Stiverne who he had previously taken the belt from, this time it was over in the first round, showing how much Wilder was growing and developing as a boxer and knockout artist. Undefeated prospect Louis Ortiz was stopped in the last round, Wilder was now ready for the biggest test in his career so far.

Deontay Wilder against Tyson Fury 'The Gypsy King' was one of the most hyped in recent years. Two undefeated fighters cut from completely different cloths. Fury the master class out fighter with incredible defensive skills and ring craft ability and Wilder with the hardest most explosive puncher in boxing at that time.

Styles makes fights and the most likely outcomes for this fight would have been Fury knocked out early or Wilder loses on points. Wilder began as usual looking for the big punch to finish it early but was outboxed by Fury in the opening rounds, he was too evasive, and Wilder could not find a gap. Fury stayed out of range for most of the fight, using his long jab to good effect. Wilder did knock down Fury in round 9 but he recovered quick and continued to dance around the ring and fire off the odd one two. It looked like Fury had the fights on points until Wilder did his specialty and fired in a gigantic right hand and left hook sending Fury flying into the canvas. He looked out cold but somehow rose from the dead to continue where he left off. It was a truly incredible fight and was scored a draw, many thought Fury had outclassed Wilder with his style but only one man hit the canvas that night.

"I think with the two knockdowns I definitely won the fight, we poured our hearts out tonight. We're both warriors, but with those two drops I think I won the fight." *Deontay Wilder.*

Regardless of judges scoring, it was an epic fight and both men left the ring still unbeaten and were to meet again. Although not before Wilder smashed through Dominic Breazeale in one round, seemingly taking out the frustration of the Fury fight. A rematch with Luiz Ortiz followed, Ortiz is a very dangerous Cuban boxer who had caused Fury problems in their previous encounter before going down in the tenth round. This time around the outcome was similar, Wilder was composed and measured using his jab to look for openings, whilst Ortiz was mixing combinations off his southpaw jab. At the beginning of the seventh round Wilder found his opening with a huge one two putting Ortiz down on the canvas. He was able to just beat the count but not could not continue.

The rematch of Wilder and Fury was eagerly anticipated and was to be a massive event after the previous controversial draw. A major difference between fights occurred when Fury changed trainers for Sugar Hill Steward from the Kronk Gym. As we have already seen, the Kronk style personified by Thomas Hearns is not an elusive defensive strategy as Fury usually adopts. It would seem impossible that Fury could change styles. What was noticeable from the outset was that both fighters were significantly heavier than ever before. This surprised many, especially Fury supporters who worried if this would affect his crafty footwork and mobility. From Wilder's perspective, it was understandable to add extra weight into those bombs, it would seem both men were coming for the knockout. While Wilder did not change his normal style, Fury did make key differences; sitting into his punches and attacking both the body and head well. Wilder's offence seemed to suffer at this onslaught and looked like a scorpion without a tail. With his balance and defence failing it was all over in the seventh round with Fury crowned the WBC Heavyweight Champion.

The story of Deontay Wilder and his future as a boxer was far from

over though. He was absolutely set on getting back to the top and taking revenge for his only loss to date.

Deontay Wilder's Style

Anyone who assumes Wilder's style to be crude, brawling without
science, is absolutely incorrect. He is likely the hardest puncher this century,
he has lightning fast and accurate hands and is an intelligent boxer. Tyson Fury
did not expose Deontay Wilder, he simply outclassed him on one night having
reinvented his entire methodology in a master class move that will be long remembered in boxing history. This should take nothing away from Wilder's past,
present and future performances and ability as an outstanding knock out artist.
Much the same as George Foreman destroying Joe Frazier and Marvin Hagler
doing the same to Thomas Hearns did not affect either man's greatness over
time.

Wilder has an extremely underrated jab, it has an accuracy rating of
30.1% in the top three of current fighters alongside Joshua and Canelo. When
he fought Ortiz it was at 43% compared to Ortiz at 29%. When Floyd Mayweather fought a UFC fighter it was still only 41%.He often used the jab to clear
the opponent's hand to land the power shot by looping his jab over their guard,
this was also a favoured tactic of the great Joe Louis. In similar style to Thomas
Hearns, Wilder would also utilise a stiff-arm jab press on his opponent's head,
to maintain distance, disrupt their balance, and act like a radar for sending in
the big shot.

Although it's Wilder's punching power that gets the job done, he
doesn't get the credit for the other skills he has. He is extremely fast for a
heavyweight, with phenomenal hand speed that make his punches like a cracking whip. He's an intelligent fighter that can set traps and make his opponent
wary of his right hand to the detriment of them forgetting about his left. Wilder
has great footwork with deceptively fast feet that are made to cut distance. His
defence is built upon excellent head movement; with the exception of the Fury
fights, he rarely gets hit.
"Back home we talk about my punches being like a whip, and the most painful
part of the whip is the tip. That's where I do my damage, right at the end of the
punches. The tip of the whip".

With Wilder's style commitment is everything, when he cracks that
whip of a right hand, along with maximum speed he must sacrifice some balance and structure to throw his entire body weight into the punch. The downside
is he is not well set up for the next punch and is vulnerable, but his priority is
simple: power.

In his stance you can observe huge rotational power as he almost
throws the jab squatting into his rear leg then leaps forward throwing his weight
through the left leg as if he has thrown a javelin. Often his rear foot will completely leave the floor, this power is boxing's equivalent of a nuclear bomb.

Using the lead leg as fulcrum creates massive force that can smash straight through an opponent's guard. There is no chance this could ever work if Wilder did not have blinding speed to produce huge velocity.

"Don't judge a book by its cover. My legs look skinny, I know, but I'm all muscle, it's all muscle, skin and bone. Think of someone like Thomas Hearns, that dude never had the biggest legs in the world but boy could he bang"
Deontay Wilder

Anthony Joshua
Record: 32 wins (27 KOs) / 4 Losses
Style: Boxer Puncher
Signature Technique: Uppercut
Famous KO: Wladimir Klitschko TKO round 11

"There are two types of warriors: the one that rides through on his horse and tries to slay everyone, and the sniper. I try to be more like the sniper. Bang. Bang. Bang. Break them down, shot by shot."
Anthony Joshua

Anthony Joshua started boxing later in life than most when he stepped into a local boxing gym in North London at the age of 20. A talented athlete who could run 100 metres at the age of 15, his rise in the art of boxing was nothing less than meteoric. Within four years his amateur record was beginning to turn heads as he rose to number three in the world. ABA and GB titles were followed by silver in the world championships, though many thought he was robbed on points in the final.

In 2012 he reached the peak of any amateur boxer by securing the Super Heavyweight gold medal at the 2012 Olympic Games in London.
The following year Joshua turned professional and won his first fight with a first-round knockout of Italian Emanuele Leo. This was followed by a succession of knockout wins until his first real test, Dillian Whyte.

Following his stunning showing at the Olympics, Joshua turned pro a year later and made his debut against Italian Emanuele Leo at The O2 Arena on October 5, 2013. He won that fight in the first round and then had 14 more straight-forward victories before being tested for the first time by Dillian Whyte.

Joshua had won the WBC international heavyweight title by knocking out Denis Bakhtov in round two, the fight with Whyte was to defend that belt. Whyte was also unbeaten and predicting an early finish to Joshua in a much-hyped fight, he had also beaten Joshua as an amateur. That time though he was fighting a very different boxer who was still a work in progress. Despite being rocked in the second round by an aggressive Whyte, Joshua dominated and finished Whyte in the seventh round with a vicious uppercut.

The following year Joshua claimed the IBF world heavyweight belt with a second round knockout of Charles Martin. He successfully defended the belt with a seventh round knockout of Dominic Breazeale.

Critics of Joshua were still claiming he had not faced a top tier boxer regardless of his undefeated eighteen wins. Wladimir Klitschko was to be just that man, an individual who had dominated the heavyweight ranks for many years until he was sensationally defeated by Tyson Fury who later vacated the belt. This fight would unite the WBA, IBO and IBF belts. Deontay Wilder still held the WBC belt.

It was a classic encounter, highly competitive and gave the fans what they wanted to see; two world class big punchers going at it. The first few rounds were slower with both fighters getting the measure of each other and feeling each other out. In the fifth round it went up a gear with Joshua adding extra pressure onto Klitschko who was knocked down, he soon responded by putting Joshua on the canvas in the next round. Klitschko looked to be in control of the fight but Joshua reverted to his solid basic fundamental boxing style. In the 11th round it looked to be Klitschko slightly ahead on points as Joshua came in for the kill knocking down the Ukrainian twice before the referee stepped in. Anthony Joshua had more than proved himself.

In 2019, Joshua was due to have his first fight in the USA, defending his IBF, WBA and WBO world heavyweight titles against Jarrell Miller on 1 June at Madison Square Garden. Miller was refused a licence to fight due to an "adverse finding" in a drug-testing sample. At six weeks' notice a replacement opponent was found in the shape of Andy Ruiz Jr a young American of Mexican heritage with 32 wins in 33 fights. Ruiz didn't look much of a fighter next to the Adonis physique of Joshua, round and chubby he looked more at home in a KFC. During the press conference Ruiz looked star struck and even asked Joshua if he could pose with his three belts, which he did. There was far less hype around this fight than the Klitschko fight and didn't compare to Wilder Vs Fury. This was expected to be a walk in the park for Joshua, another day in the office. Ruiz, however, with zero level of pressure and expectations on him, had very different ideas.

It was a remarkable fight and a gigantic upset with Ruiz flooring Joshua four times and stopping him in the seventh round. Ruiz took the belts and broke Joshua's unbeaten record. This was no freak lucky punch win though. Ruiz is an aggressive forward pressing infighter who had Joshua on the back foot from the offset, totally unable to handle him. At one point he caught Ruiz with a left hook which put him down briefly in the third round but the Mexican returned fire knocking Joshua down twice in the round. The atmosphere in the arena soon turned as it became evident the unthinkable was occurring. It was over for Joshua in round seven when he spat out his gum shield whilst being down on all fours. This was the biggest boxing upset since James 'Buster' Douglas knocked out Mike Tyson and unbelievable to many fans.

Once again styles make fights and Joshua had failed to prepare adequately for this fight and had clearly written off Ruiz as cannon fodder. There was also something different about Joshua that night, he did not look himself. Immediately following the fight his father was seen having harsh words with promoter and manager Eddie Hearn, what was said and what happened we may never know.

The rematch 6 months later was a very different affair. Joshua fought a completely different fight, using his footwork and lead hand to control the ring, he immobilised a surprisingly worse shaped Ruiz. It was a measured performance with Joshua showing respect to Ruiz and taking no chances. Although Ruiz was cut early on Joshua played things out patiently. Joshua used his jab to good effect to keep Ruiz at bay. It was a unanimous decision.

"I just wanted to put on a great boxing masterclass and also show the sweet science of this lovely sport. It's about hitting and not getting hit"
Anthony Joshua.

Boxing along with most things was severely impacted by Covid 19 in 2020 but Joshua did manage to have one defence of his titles in December, against dangerous hard hitting Kubrat Pulev. It was a spirited performance from Joshua who was demonstrating vastly improved footwork and defence, he knocked out Pulev in round 9, only his second loss since losing to Wladimir Klitschko in the past.

In March 2021 contracts were signed and agreed for a Joshua Vs Fury bout, , including an immediate rematch clause. At the time of writing this is the fight everyone wants to see and it looks set to be an epic clash of the titans.

Anthony Joshua's Style
Many have criticised the technique and style of Anthony Joshua of being somewhat stiff and robotic, much like they had twenty years earlier of fellow Brit and hard hitter Frank Bruno. Both look like bodybuilders, can definitely hit but appear to have flaws in their armoury, much the same as Earnie Shavers who never won the title. A major difference when comparing Joshua to a Bruno or Shavers, is that regardless of era the man accomplished much more in a shorter time period with an out-standing record. From Olympic gold medallist to 24 wins in 25 fights and 22 knockouts. Be under no illusion Anthony Joshua is an excellent boxer who uses a minimalistic and fundamental control of the basics in his style and has an extremely potent knock-out ability.

As a boxer puncher Joshua seeks to make maximum use of his size, strength and athletic ability. He has a mastery of the basic building blocks of boxing and an excellent jab, which he uses well to set up power shots. Joshua has a tight and disciplined defence rarely dropping his guard at any time. He has fast agile footwork and uses this well to enter in and out and circle his opponent.

The Jab
Joshua has a highly underrated jab; it sets up everything he does, and he frequently employs a one two combination to pressurise his opponent and keep distance. In the rematch with Andy Ruiz Jr the jab was central to his strategy and it kept Ruiz well away and controlled both the pace and distance of the fight.

Footwork

Again, Joshua's footwork is very textbook and clinical, he is mobile and quick; rarely in one spot long. He bobs in and out, testing with the jab and also enjoys circling his opponent. Joshua is extremely good at creating angles from the pivot and by side stepping, from here he can accurately place both the uppercut and hook.

Counterpunching

Joshua is an exceptional counter puncher, and this allows him to compete at the highest level. He uses his height and reach to maximum advantage and this allows him to block and use subtle head movement whilst still being in position to retaliate at long range. He steps in deep to the opponent and is able to intercept. Unusually, Joshua often uses a lead hook to counter a jab, this is a technique from the past and was a signature move of the great Joe Frazier.

Anthony Joshua definitely does not get the credit he deserves as a world champion, he has accomplished much in a relatively short period of time and proved himself a worthy top-class fighter. With the exception of the first Ruiz fight he never has an off day and improves fight on fight. The Ruiz loss and subsequent revenge was a great lesson for him in adaptation and forced him to go back to the drawing board to upgrade his skills. He is an accurate and powerful puncher; his 88% knockout rate is outstanding. Whatever the result between the Gypsy King and AJ, we are guaranteed to see a great fight with two class fighters of very different schools.

'It takes a certain type of man to become a boxer, to fight for a living. To be able to have the confidence to hit another man, to control your fears. You must overcome the physical aspect and believe in the art, the discipline of the sport. You need to study. You need to be smart.'
Anthony Joshua

Above: Anthony Joshua

Chapter Eight: Fighting Stance

The stance in boxing was at one time referred to as the 'on guard' The orthodox position is typically used for right-handed fighters who lead with the left hand and foot and keep the dominant hand back to deliver the strongest blows. The southpaw position is the opposite of this and typically used by left-handed fighters. Very advanced boxers use both positions and can switch accordingly. It is also rare but known that some right-hand boxers prefer to place their strongest hand forward in a southpaw position and the same for some southpaw boxers.

Regardless of the above it would make sense for every boxer to first master the basic on guard from either a right or left lead before experimenting with variations.

Main Points:

- The body is turned sideward, this is both defensive, by giving the opponent a smaller target, and offensive by placing the right hand in a stronger and more hidden position to deliver a knockout punch.

- The chin is tucked in and down behind the left shoulder, this provides a wall of defence when delivering the left jab.
- The left (lead) foot points forward towards the opponent and is flat on the floor. It should be able to glide forward and transfer the body weight timed with either a left or right hand.

- The right (rear) foot is turned sideward, this opens the hip to turn with maximum twist when the right hand is delivered. The heel is raised on both feet when moving, stepping or shuffling.

- The knees are bent at all times. They should be bent enough to engage all the muscles of the lower body in a feeling of springiness but not so low as to restrict mobility and fatigue the muscles.

- The distance between the feet should be wide enough to be balanced and stable but not too far or it reduces mobility, the actual distance will depend on the height of the boxer.

- The elbows are down and tucked in against the ribs, this provides protection but also the base to launch fast and powerful un-telegraphed punches.

- The hands are held high to the face, forming a shield and a position to deliver quick blows. The front hand is more in front of the shoulder and the rear is close to the chin.

- The weight should be slightly forward. This provides a stronger base for impact and less telegraphed movement needed to put weight behind your punch.

- The head should never move by itself but in unity with the body. Both arms should always be relaxed.

- The stance is never static, it is always moving. This does not mean unnecessary 'dancing' or expenditure of energy but more continuous shuffling of the feet and co-ordinated small circles with the hands.

- This serves to both keep the opponent guessing and make you harder to hit but also more importantly it allows you to spring into action from any angle very quickly.

- Think of an animal stalking its prey, it will never stand fixed and static it will slowly move and circle and engage its body in preparation for an explosive attack. Always keep your eyes on your opponent and maintain your guard.

    Below are two useful exercises to practice checking that stance positioning is correct, if these can be done correctly without losing balance the stance is good.

1. Raise up onto the balls of the feet and then lower down into a deep squat, repeat several times.

2. Much like a weave, bend forward and backward from the hips.

Chapter Nine: Footwork

"Remember, it's always good to throw the punch where you could hit him and he can't hit you. That's what the science of boxing is all about."
Cus D'Amato

Footwork is everything in boxing. It is the most difficult skill to master and once achieved it will serve to add venom to punches and elusiveness to your defence. To be able to recognise both when and where to move is the basis of great skill in boxing.

Great boxing technique and punching is reliant on being balanced, light on the feet and graceful. Hopping, jumping and leaping around wastes energy and compromises balance. The overall aim of footwork is to mislead your opponent, tire them out and keep you out of danger.

Depending on distance, heels will raise when further away from your opponent and acting defensively. When the gap is closed, and you are 'in fighting,' the foot will need to be in contact with the floor to produce greater force by distribution of weight.

The legs should never cross in boxing, a good guide to remember is to move the foot closest to the direction you wish to move first. This ensures you maintain the on guard position for balance, stability and the ability to hit.

From An Orthodox Stance:

- To move forward, the left foot moves first.
- To move backward, the right foot moves first.
- To move left, the left foot moves first
- To move right, the right foot moves first.

For linear movement the upper body should be relatively upright and the on guard held at all times.

For lateral movement a slight lean with the upper body in the direction of the step adds speed and takes the head off the firing line for defence and providing a favourable angle to punch.

The steps themselves should be short and quick, never overreach and step long. Boxing stepping is often referred to as sliding. If the step is too big we lose the balance and connection of the body, likewise if the foot is dragged it creates unnecessary resistance and loss of speed and mobility.

Sliding enables you to maintain stable, whole-body kinetic energy in the on guard position, therefore when you move forward with the left foot you are pushing off the right foot and the same in moving back you move back with the right foot by pushing off the left. This method of moving very much serves to set up the mechanics of hitting anddelivering power.

Remember: THE FEET ARE CONNECTED TO THE HANDS AT ALL TIMES.

Pivoting is another important skill to master within footwork, the pivot is used in place of a sliding step to move the body laterally and change the angle relative to the opponent; this can be for both offensive and defensive reasons. The pivot is instigated by pressing through the ball of the front foot whilst quickly stepping laterally with the rear foot. This is a useful movement at close range, which can produce just a small amount of space by changing one's angle to the opponent to effectively deliver and evade a blow.

The stance switch is a more advanced movement in which the boxer can change stances mid combination. This can be unpredictable and hard to read for the opponent; particularly during in fighting when attacking the body.

The Steel Rod Principle

In boxing a large component of power generation is produced by pivoting the body around a central axis. This central pivot is like an engine and the arms are the drivers of force.

Chapter Ten: The Left Jab

In Boxing the jab is the king of all punches and has its roots back to the origins of the art. It does not just score points; it is the movement that sets up the killer punch. The jab should neither be considered basic nor be the first weapon one should learn in boxing; the stance and footwork should always come first – the building will collapse without the foundations.

The jab, when used correctly, will control the opponent and the fight. Being able to land the jab means you can land every other punch. Although not a knockout punch, the jab can still cause considerable damage over the course of a round.

To become a good boxer this punch must be fully mastered, but it is not to be wholly relied upon. Without conviction and technique, it is worthless, but performed correctly it can make the difference between victory and defeat.

The First Three Important Points:

- Fully Extend the arm – like cracking a whip, allow the power to transfer right through.

- Lean slightly to the right – this removes your head off the centre line to avoid a jab counter.

- Tuck the chin into the shoulder and head turned slightly to the right – this protects against a right-hand counter.

Two Main Types Of Jab:

1. Flick jab – fast and crisp, difficult to see coming but limited power due to arm only movement.

2. Power jab – full body force, with long extension of the shoulder coupled with a step and shift of body weight, very powerful but easier to see coming and a harder position to quickly recover from.

Methods Of Delivery:

- With a body left feint; a quick movement towards the opponent's centre followed immediately by a crisp jab.

- Step right, move the body forward and down then straighten up quickly with a jab and sharp shoulder twist.

- Fake a right hand to the body then switch positions fully to the right and fire a hard jab.

- The postman's knock. A double left extremely useful against fast opponents. Deliver the first punch with a left step and right follow step, the second punch comes with a second left step. The footwork combination ensures you are very quickly smothering your opponents' range and hitting with full power.

- Left hook set up. Hit 2 or 3 long range fast but not full power left hooks, your opponent will be focussed on lateral defence as you suddenly step forward with a full force jab.

The Body Jab

This is an effective movement to damage the body over a sequence of hits, the target area is larger and more static than the head. The solar plexus is the ideal place to hit.

Chapter Eleven: The Straight Right

The cross or straight right is a power punch in boxing and used to damage and knock out the opponent. Speed is essential to ensure success in this punch. Transference of weight from left to right leg is needed to generate power and hit straight through the target, retracting quickly back to the guard. Balance and leverage are very important to perform this punch well, otherwise you will be merely "arm punching"

Main Points:

- Twist and reverse the shoulders fully, Jack Dempsey called this the whirling shoulder. By doing this, it adds torque from the waist and hips and also removes the head from the centre line.

- Take a small step with the left to transfer weight and power and raise the right heel slightly to extend reach and leverage.

- Keep the left hand up by the chin and elbow tucked to the ribs.

- Imagine cracking a whip with a fast retraction, this punch should be loose full of snap and crispness.

- Twist and corkscrew the fist so it lands palm facing down.

- At the moment of impact contract the abdominal area as if doing a sit up to add even more power.

- Do not just throw the punch to the opponent's face, aim at a very specific target and deliver with full precision.

- Never forget to always begin side on, this enables the full shoulder rotation to occur for maximum power.

- Although usually thrown after a left hand, occasionally it is acceptable to lead with the right hand, especially when the opponent is tired or at the beginning of an encounter with the element of surprise.

- Always remember to drive through the legs and anchor the feet, imagine a pulley from your right fist to right foot, one doesn't move without the other.

Chapter Twelve: The Right Hook

A powerful punch that can produce huge momentum but is more challenging to hit and catch the opponent with. Many fighters avoid practicing this punch as it is harder to do it correctly than others. It should never be a wide 'haymaker'.

Correct Mechanics:

- Snap the left shoulder back violently, slightly dropping it as you raise the right heel.

- The arc of the arm should be tight and controlled as it fires out relaxed. Then for a split second stiffen the hand, wrist, elbow and shoulder as one at the point of impact.

- Release any tension and retract the arm as fast as it went out. The shoulders and waist power the arm in and out, not the arm itself.

Contrary to popular belief this is not best as a long-range attack but at short range (a Mike Tyson speciality) where it is more difficult to see and hard to intercept. For example:

- A one-two, off the back of a hard jab, stepping in with the right leg.

- Coming in and out of a clinch.

- As a counter to the jab step in and to the left of the opponent then send in the hook.

At close range there is also opportunity to throw a right body hook which can cause a great deal of damage to the ribs, for example:

- Throw a long left hook to the head, when the opponents guard raises hit with the hook to his ribs under his elbows.

- Slip the jab then step and hook to the ribs.

Chapter Thirteen: The Left Hook

A classic punch, which has the benefit of being fast and hard to read but also versatile at long and short ranges. With the correct mechanics it is possible to deliver a lot of weight and power with this punch.

It is a punch that demands accuracy, do not aim for the cheek, head or ear – go for the side of the chin, that is the sleeping tablet. The left hook can be a countering blow and a finisher.

Although the straight right is the most common knockout punch, many great fighters have made the left hook their go-to finisher. It is also harder to see and defend against.

Main Points:

- Leave the arm in guard, turn the body to the right whilst shifting the weight to the right leg.

- Throw the left arm in an arc and through the opponent driving with the knuckles.

- The punch should be a snap, driving body weight not arm power. It is critical to transfer the power and momentum from the legs and hips into the punch.

- Imagine there is a pole from your left fist running through your hip to left foot. You are fixed to the floor through this pole. The only way to move your left hand is the move the left hips.

Opportunities For Delivery:

- Immediately following checking your opponent's jab.

- Hit with a left jab to the body then left hook to the head.

- Double left hook, first to the body then to the head.

- As one two, particularly effective at longer range to confuse the opponent.

- Reverse of above to set a strong powerful jab after the hook.

Chapter Fourteen: Uppercut

One of the harder punches to pull off and use effectively but once mastered is both dangerous and punishing. The biggest issue is making it natural and fluid, the harder a person tries to make this punch connect, the less it works out. It can be used at short range and mid-range, though short is easier. The perfect time is when your opponent rushes in bending forward, head down.

The uppercut is somewhat of a surprise punch and difficult to defend against, when it lands it drives the opponents head straight up which can be devastating. The key to the mechanics is to use a lifting motion of the shoulder whilst straightening the legs, for extra power spring onto the toes.

Main Points:

*   For a right uppercut, bend to the right and slightly forward, drop the right arm 3-4 inches with the fingers facing the body. Bring the arm up in an underhand arc to the opponent's chin, the twist in the right hip adds power.

*   For a left uppercut, it is similar to the right but using the left side of the body, ensure to keep the free arm close to the chest as a guard.

*   Keep the arm relaxed, snap the punch upward, driving up with the legs, the force comes from the ground not the arm.

Other Opportunities To Use The Uppercut:

*   Slip to the inside of the jab making sure you step in quickly before firing a quick uppercut.

*   Counter a right cross by slipping to the right with a left uppercut, be sure to turn the head to the right.

*   Left uppercut to the liver, this was a favourite punch of the great Gene Tunney.

*   Right uppercut to the body, works well on a crouching opponent stepping in.

Chapter Fifteen: The Overhand Right

A more unusual long-range attack, the time taken to reach its destination is compensated by the tremendous power potential of this punch.
It is a momentum punch so should be delivered from long range with the body forward and to the left slightly, brace the abdominals hard. Turn the wrist all the way over to avoid damaging the hand.

This is a useful punch against a tall defensive boxer who leans back. The best time to catch him is when he straightens back up, footwork is the key to the delivery. Make sure the left hand covers the face and do not lean back as the same punch could be delivered straight back at you.

Short Version:

This is another surprise attack not be utilised too often. Usually stepping in with the jab then bring a bent short right arm over the top as a surprising but very powerful hit. It is possible to add a lot of weight through this punch with good torque and dropping the bodyweight.

Chapter Sixteen: Developing Punching Combinations

It is easier to defend against one punch than a sequence of punches. In most boxing fights the knockout is not the result of the first blow but more often the second, third or even fourth punch. This is not coincidental, the sequence of a combination is often pre-determined to lead to that outcome. By mastering several key combinations in your own style will serve you extremely well in fighting. Of course, in real time those combinations will be delivered from different angles and with differing timing, depending on the opponent and what they do.

The one-two and various variations of it are a great place to start and you should gain mastery here before moving on to more complex and advanced combinations.

It is important to integrate and use the mind; before beginning any sequence in training run through it in your head and work through all the body mechanics and adjustments, this visualisation will help enormously.

Combinations themselves are endless with a huge number of possibilities for a 5 or 6 punch combination. Also remember the changes in power on each punch within a combination has an endless changing quality to them. You may start hard, go light, then end hard again, or all of them could be hard or it could gradually increase in power step by step.

The more punches you throw the better, but they must have a specific purpose and target not just a combination thrown without focus. By utilising punches in a specific order, it's like a magic combination increasing the possibility of each single punch to hit its target. It has been said before that boxing is like a game of chess, one punch will set up the next move and the one that follows that. Never wait between punches, the delay achieves nothing and leaves you vulnerable. A combination is like what it says it is, it's the key to unlocking the safe and taking the money.

Here are some basic combinations to get started:

One-two Punch

This is a classic combination which can be used to both dominate and win fights. It does not always need to be both punches to the head, a left to the head followed by a right to the body can be devasting in consequence along with a left to the body and right to the head.

Often the first punch is lighter in power but fast and crisp, it is designed to allow you to enter in range with your feet to follow up with the finisher. It is worth investing many hours to practice this combination, the key is to not apply too much force in the first blow, and to spin the shoulders into the second.

Another superb delivery method is the double jab followed by the right. There should be stepping on every punch, the best timing is jab, pause and then jab/cross. Some fighters hold the last jab for a split second as a measurement gauge before the right, this can work but again not to be used every time.

Defensively, a small movement of head and body to the left as you deliver the right along with turning the arm down and in slightly is a great counter to a jab in return. Bobbing and weaving in between any one two combination should keep you well out of trouble.

Step forward with the left foot delivering a jab to block the opponent's vision, immediately step forward with the right foot and snap a right punch to the chin. This action must be at high speed and deadly accurate.

The stepping with the jab is essential to ensure you can hit with the right, it is a test of measurement, unless your opponent comes to you then you can remain static and catch him on the way in.

Double Left Hook

The double hook, first one to the body, second one to the head is a favourite of infighters like Mike Tyson and Joe Frazier. This double act perfectly demonstrates a combination that works to increase the success rate of the next punch. Once the first hard body hook has hit it is natural for the opponent to bring the elbow down, thereby exposing their head. A lovely combination when it comes off, it is unexpected because most fighters combine punches with alternate hands. Used too frequently it is easily blocked and countered so dish it out sparingly.

Right Uppercut Left Hook

A wonderful combination when it can be landed, these two punches go together like fish and chips. Once the right uppercut lands the hook falls into place. The opponent's head is driven up and back and in a perfect position to land the left hook. This combination is very difficult to defend against. The timing needs to be perfect, with full speed and no delay between the punches. The uppercut once landed causes great confusion and shock and is perfect to set up the hook. Another variation is left uppercut and left hook, this is equally devastating.

Left Jab Right Cross Left Hook

The one, two, three. This is a great combination because each punch sets up the mechanics for the next allowing you to store kinetic energy generated from one punch to unload into the next one. You step into the job, twist and rotate into the right throwing the weight into the left leg and pivoting on the right leg. You would normally be slightly off balance now but instead you use this momentum to take into the hook by shifting all the weight to the right leg and snapping in the hook.

Chapter Seventeen: Body Punching

Every boxing punch can be used as an attack to the body as well as the head. Body punching is severely neglected in modern boxing but was well trained and practiced in the golden area and recognised as a valuable and necessary method of offense. When you observe a liver shot hit the target you know how devasting this can be, most fighters would rather be hit on the chin than the liver. Apart from ending a fight, body punching also wears down the opponent and takes their toll. They diminish stamina, balance, confidence and most importantly open up possibilities for the head shot. There is an old saying in boxing "if you hurt the body the head will come to you".

The body is a larger target than the head, it is impossible to miss, your opponent can not slip a body shot. Continuous shots and the guard will begin to drop. It's like continuously putting money into the bank; you are making a future investment.

It's useful to learn some basic anatomical knowledge like Bob Fitzsimons and Jimmy Wilde did, as a guide for punch placement:

- For hooks aim for the side Infront of the kidney and of course the liver and upper rib cage.

- The uppercut should be aimed at the pit of the stomach.

- Jabs and crosses directly to the solar plexus

Hooks and crosses should always be thrown on the inside and remember to bend your knees to drive from the floor. The distance should be closer than head punching but not too close to avoid getting smothered. You still need room to unload. Perfect the art of body punching and you will have a formidable tool in your arsenal. Perhaps not as showy as headhunting but to be able to body snatch will serve any boxer very well.

Chapter Eighteen: In-fighting

A whole book could be devoted to mastering in-fighting. To be effective and dangerous at close quarters range is very important and many fighters like Frazier and Duran based their whole style on it. Although perhaps not as picturesque as a long right shot hitting the target, there is still something very beautiful about seeing a tight hook or uppercut destroy an opponent. It is not easy to keep a good in-fighter at distance, and once inside the opponent's inability to fight effectively will be a massive handicap. Many in-fighters don't mind taking a bit of punishment to get into range and once there like to work the body. As we have seen, body punishment is both cumulative and debilitating. Getting in is key, through footwork and of course slipping punches and bobbing and weaving to avoid punishment and loading up your own punches. It is amazing the power that can be generated at close range, especially with the right mechanics. Driving with the legs and twisting the shoulders is even more important at close range. Working with less space, everything needs to be honed.

Methods To Get In:

1. From a jab, slip left, step forward quickly with the left foot followed by the right. Place your forehead on the opponent's chest or left shoulder and fire in as many short-range shots as possible. Twist the shoulders as much as possible and "feel" with the arms where the opponent is going - to stick to him and detect openings. When you uppercut rise on the toes, keep getting into the inside position, when the opponent retreats follow him quickly.

2. Once you can get into the inside position you will have the advantage. In response to a hook, it is simple to step inside with a straight guard then dropping the hands almost chopping over the opponent's guard to smother them. Once you can control like this you can sneak in short range punches. The wrists and elbows will be used to pin and prevent counter attacks, keep contact, stick and follow his arms.

3. Another entry technique against a body shot (hook or straight) is to step in with straight guard again, cover on the inside and uppercut with the other hand. It needs to be fast, any fighter not up for this range will press on the biceps and push you away.

The pressing down on the opponent's biceps can also be used if you get into trouble infighting, do this and spring back out. As an in-fighter when this happens you can deal with it two ways.

1. Twist each of your gloves up and onto the opponent's wrists or forearms, this will prevent him being able to hook or uppercut and you can step out.

2. In this position the opponent's thumbs are on the inside, you can apply shock by tensing your body rising upwards then totally relax as you drop down around six inches then you can quickly fire out hooks.

When the opponent puts pressure on you to push himself away, do not push back in retaliation, relax step back and again this is the point to unleash a well times hook to the chin.

Chapter Nineteen: Feinting and Drawing

Feinting is the art of misleading your opponent to think you're about to do something that you aren't. The second he tries to defend the feint; you attack with something else. For example, make it look like a jab but throw a left hook, look like you are going the body but go to the head.

Feinting creates openings and openings are what is needed for punching to be successful. To be good at feinting you need to understand the opponent and how they react; of course, every opponent reacts differently. Again, this is why boxing is like chess; it is strategic. You can unlock the opponent's game by using feints, find out what moves him left and right and how he defends and counter-punches. It is like setting a trap to catch him later. It's very tough and demoralising is someone can predict what you are about to do.

The feint doesn't just have to be in the body movement, the eyes can feint too, look at his body but hit the head. Some fighters are more susceptible to feints than others; the key is to use it to create opportunities to land focused, accurate and powerful punches that are impossible to defend against. It used to be said in old school boxing that the first man to reveal his method of attack is the man likely to lose. There is some truth to this and certainly rushing in without a plan is an extremely poor strategy. Speed is critical in feinting, there can be no hesitation once the feint is thrown before the combination is launched. Failure to act quickly and the opportunity will be missed.

A draw is to fake an opening or gap for your opponent to punch at, set up ready for you to counter. An example is dropping the right hand to provoke the opponent to jab but being ready to defend and counter with your right body hook. You can also draw a right cross by dropping your left hand. Dropping hands lower can draw your opponent into hitting high and vice versa. It can be one way to trap the opponent to getting inside your range. Generally, most in-fighters don't do this though because of the potential risk and prefer to push forward. If you are going to use drawing, make sure it does not backfire and you get caught.

Chapter Twenty: Counter Punching

Counter punching can produce some of the most devastating punches in boxing because the force of the punch is increased by the opponent coming towards you, like two cars in a head on collision. Counter punching is also making the opponent miss his punch, making him pay for mistakes. Anticipation and awareness play a huge role in counter punching, as does timing and patience. Again, like a game of chess the same movement may not work two times in a row, you need to use creativity and intelligence.

Here are some standard counter blows from the old school:

- From an incoming left jab, step forward with your left foot slipping your head to the right and sending in a left hook

- Against the jab again, step in with the guard high catching the jab in the right hand whilst returning a jab

- Change around the above pattern by stepping in with the left foot and using the left hook. You will need to slip further to the right and power can be added by a short follow step with the right foot

- In a reply to a left jab step in with the left foot with the head moving to left off the centerline. Use an overhand right to come over the top of your opponent's arm, be sure to keep the left hand high

- A short right punch held close to your body can be delivered straight to the opponent's heart in response to a jab, you must step in and hit with a vertical fist thumb up

- Against a jab to the body use 'the stop' - pull in your abdomen, quickly lean forward and send in either a left or right

- Against a right cross, move to your right and forward stepping in with the left foot and send in a left handed uppercut to the liver

Chapter Twentyone: Style In Fighting

All fighters need to develop their style, regardless of the art being practiced. What is style? It is perfect balance, concise and coordinated movements of the hands and body, removing any extra and unnecessary movements, perfect timing of delivering blows, ability to dodge or avoid an attack with a millimetre to spare. There is a cleanness and a springiness to all actions that make the movements crisp, flawless and give the appearance of effortlessness and efficiency.

Style in fighting gives great preference to sharp angular straight attacks. Whilst lateral movements do have their place, they are in the minority compared to a straight punch, as a straight line will always beat a circle.

Style is also demonstrated when all the joints, muscles and tissues of the body coordinate into each attack, with full body power. The feet glide effortlessly, like dancers on ice, carrying the full weight of the body into each strike.

Perfect timing is required to deliver a knockout, the opponent must be either static or moving in, not backward. Great style in fighting will enable the exponent to control their opponent's movements, dictate to him his next move, force him to make mistakes and punish him in return.

Style takes intelligence and 'fighting IQ', an ability to read opponents and understand himself, like a game of chess. In developing an individual style to achieve all of the above one must be aware and play to one's strengths and abilities, the style should also reflect the personality, temperament and physique of the fighter.

Finally, great style is about mastery of a set of basic techniques, the adage 'less is more' applies tenfold in boxing. Great skill is the result of deep correct practice of few things, to be able to do five things to absolute perfection far exceeds doing many things averagely. Although the fighter must have a broad range of knowledge, he must also be a specialist, never a jack of all trades, he must be a master of his own style.

119

Chapter Twentytwo: The Kronk

The Kronk Gym is a place where champions have been made and fighters are reborn and upgraded. The Kronk gym is also the place fighters go to learn how to use their power and skill to produce the knockout blow. It is renowned for a signature style of a strong left jab behind crashing venomous right hands. Some of the best knock out artists in the world have been through the doors of the Kronk. The list of Kronk Champions includes:

Dennis Andries, Thomas Hearns, Eddie Mustafa Muhammad, Leeonzer Barber, Evander Holyfield, Welcome N'cita, Jesse Benevides, John David Jackson, Jimmy Paul, Mark Breland, Hilmer Kenty, Aaron Pryor, Gaby Canizales, Lennox Lewis, Lucia Rijker, Julio Cesar Chavez, Oliver McCall, Graciano Rocchigiani, Oscar De La Hoya, Mike McCallum, Leon Spinks, Jeff Fenech, Gerald Mc-Clellan, Duane Thomas, Miguel Angel Gonzalez, Milton McCrory, Tony Tucker, Naseem Hamed, Michael Moorer, Johnathon Banks and Andy Lee.
Top professionals who have trained there includes:
Henry Akinwande, Muhammad Ali, Kenny Gould, Matthew Saad Muhammad, Alexis Arguello, Trevor Berbick, Courtney Hooper, Rick Roufus, Tyrell Biggs, Cassius Clay Horne, Jesus Ruiz, Cedric Boswell, J.L. Ivey, Keitoku Senrima, Donald Bowers, Derrick Jefferson, Omar Shieka, David Braxton, Tom Johnson, Hurley Snead, Mark Breland, Anthony Jones, Kenny Snow, Shannon Briggs, Frank Williams, Taurrek Fikes, Floyd Mayweather Sr. ,Jeremy Williams, George Foreman, Oliver McCall, Lance Williams, Tony Fulilangi, Damon McCreary, Greg Wright, Boyd Gardner, Jr. Bronco McKart, Mark Rowe, , Vitali Klitschko, Wladmir Klitschko, Dennis Andries, Migel Cotto, Kermit Cintron, Jermine Taylor, Oscar De la Hoya, Lennox Lewis and Tyson Fury.
And many others................

They came to be trained, coached, instructed and mentored by but one man who knew the ways of old school boxing; a certain Emmanuel Steward. Steward began his boxing journey in his hometown of Detroit at the home gym of Joe Louis and Sugar Ray Robinson. The two trainers Jimmy Myland and Festus Rice tutored him in solid basics and fundamentals of the old school ways. He was a promising boxer with talent and drive and won back-to-back junior titles and became a successful golden gloves fighter. A pivotal moment in his life was in 1963 during a championship fight when he was losing and abandoned the advice of his corner to fight defensively against an aggressive pressing opponent. Instead, he went on the front foot and won the fight in a shocking turn of events. This became central to the philosophy of the Kronk, with Steward believing that to obtain the most out of life, and to succeed at the very highest level, one must be willing to take risks combined with determination, discipline and sacrifice.

The Kronk gym began with Steward coaching his younger brother in the early part of 1970 , five months later he was also a golden gloves fighter. Unbelievably Emanuel Steward has trained and/or managed over 40 world-champion boxers. He mentored Thomas The Hitman Hearns during most of his career and it is he who perhaps epitomises the whipping, pistol like fluidity in punching that is a trademark of this gym.

Hearns's great rival Sugar Ray Leonard was also a regular visitor to the Kronk and had been trained by Steward in the early part of his career to win Olympic gold. With Heavyweight big punchers Steward excelled in bringing out the very best traits in them. When Evander Holyfield asked him to train him to fight Riddick Bowe, Holyfield was a huge underdog. Bowe was bigger with a superior jab and could fight both on the inside and outside. Steward re-trained Holyfield on the fundamentals of the sweet science with a focus on his balance and footwork to ensure he was placing his feet in the right position and correctly timing his punches. Holyfield regained the title he had lost and was a new fighter, with rhythm and precision in his arsenal. Lennox Lewis was reborn under Steward and went on to become a complete fighter and one of the greatest heavyweights of his generation. Steward became the 'hired gun' for top fighters to improve and upgrade. Sports illustrated named him 'Mr Fix it'.

Following Stewards death in 2012 the Kronk Gym continues under his prodigy, Emmanuel's nephew Sugarhill Steward. Following in his uncle's footsteps. Sugarhill was contacted in 2019 by a certain Tyson Fury to train him for a world title rematch with Deontay Wilder. Wilder a huge puncher had stolen a draw from Fury a year earlier. A clever, classy, defensive boxer Fury won the rematch in February 2020 by technical knockout in the 7th round. Fury's style was transformed into aggressive punching with venom and it was one of the biggest upsets in recent years. The young Steward had followed his uncles' blueprint and trained Fury on technique and developing knockout ability. A decade earlier Emmanuel Steward had met a young Fury and seen tremendous potential in him; his nephew Sugarhill commented after the Wilder win: "Emanuel Steward is smiling down from heaven. He knew Tyson Fury would become a champion way back then."

Chapter Twentythree: Is Bigger Always Better?

If we consider Newton's second law of physics:
The acceleration of an object as produced by a net force is directly proportional to the magnitude of the net force, in the same direction as the net force, and inversely proportional to the mass of the object.

This equation can be simply rearranged as force equals mass multiplied by acceleration. With boxing it means that an object with a greater mass (heavier person) will produce more force (the punch) compared to a smaller mass if they are travelling with the same acceleration.

This is of course a scientifically proven fact and not to be disputed, all things considered a 200 pound man will generally hit harder than a 140 pound man. However, 'all things being considered' still leaves some grey areas. There will always be exceptions to this (the weight question, not the physics) and even a potential 'cap' at weight when it comes to boxing power.
In training for the 2000 Olympic games Team USA measured the power of all their boxers using sensors on the bags, the highest scores were recorded by Jeff Lacy. He weighed 165 pounds, but there were super heavyweights being analysed who weighed over 220 pounds, this is a strange result, how can it be explained?

I would suggest that weight, whilst an important part of the punching power equation, is not the most important ingredient - the connection in the body to integrate all joints, muscles and tissue efficiently and effectively is. Therefore, it is reasonable to suggest that from a boxing perspective a lightweight fighter could hit as hard as a middleweight and a middleweight as hard as a heavyweight. Certainly, in the world of boxing super heavyweight 250 pound plus fighters have never been the heaviest hitters. I believe there is a limit whereby being too large restricts the coordination and crispness to connect the body so it delivers with full power. The most explosive hardest hitters in the history of boxing have been the smaller men, Fitzsimmons, Dempsey, Langford, Louis, Marciano and more recently Tyson.

Nat Fleischer, one of boxing's most prolific writers and historians, collated data on the physiques of 470 heavyweight fighters. Results indicated that weight, girth (height/weight), reach and thigh measurements correlated strongest with the fighters with the most wins and KO percentages. This indicates that there are multiple factors at bay. The thigh demonstrates the theory of power transferred through the legs from the ground.

It is my own opinion in these multitude of factors that a number of traits are needed to hit hard, some can be taught others are hereditary. So, the most powerful fighter will be genetically gifted, well taught, be intelligent enough to synthesise and understand their teaching and of course, have an outstanding work ethic.
Those genetic and acquired abilities to punch hard would include:

- Technique
- Co-ordination
- Balance
- Speed
- Snap & follow through
- Timing
- Intent

Force=mass x acceleration. So, less mass with more speed could apply more force than a slower but heavier mass. A big guy might be slower. Also, it is the mass involved in the punch that is important. This is where the coordination of the body to deliver whole-body power means technique can conquer brute strength. A heavy arm still has less mass than a small person! This is why a stiff, stepping jab hurts more than a flicking jab even though the arm movement is the same.

Also, it is not only important to coordinate all the punching muscles, it is also important not to involve muscles that hinder the punch. This is why being tense has a detrimental effect on power and the importance of mental training to maintain relaxed movement during the ferocity of a boxing match.

Chapter Twentyfour: Science In Boxing

The art of punching is a complex interaction of body segment movements from the feet to the hand. Each segment contributes to the increased velocity of the subsequent segment to allow the ballistic action of performing the punch to be accomplished in an efficient manner.

Firstly, we need to differentiate between just a hard punch and an effective punch. Think about the punching ball used in travelling circuses to measure power. When it is hit the aim is to produce as much power as possible to turn the dial and achieve the highest possible score. There is no concern for being counter hit, being able to hit a second time and indeed to be in any kind of recoverable position thereafter.

With an effective punch we need to produce maximum power whilst maintaining balance, composure, while being aware of our opponent's potential defence and counter. Also, the punch is more often included in a combination of various other punches.

Effective punching is efficient use of the body to throw the punch. Effective punching is the least amount of wasted effort necessary to achieve the desired result.

The two primary components at work in throwing a punch are strength and mechanics. When strength and mechanics work together well there is an effective transfer of momentum from all parts of the body into the fist.

A common criticism of weak punching is 'all arm'. By definition this is throwing a punch using the power and weight of the arm only, with no body momentum. In contrast, if the major joints and muscles of the body have worked together and produced the necessary momentum the arm will merely be the delivery system of the engine, acting like a whip driving the end of the punch into the opponent. If arm strength is used alone the punch will become disconnected and the arm will lose its ability to receive and transfer the momentum and kinetic energy from the body into the punch.

This disconnection forces the arm-shoulder complex to become more active than it should in terms of throwing a punch. This typically happens when the person is trying to make up for the lack of efficient transfer of momentum by "muscling" the punch.

To analyse the correct punching process requires an understanding of the kinetic chain or sequence. When we are talking about using the body to throw a punch we are talking about the kinetic chain.

In a boxing cross the upper body and hips rotate fully around a central axis This central pivot is like an engine and the arms are the drivers of force.

The kinetic chain/sequence is the development and transfer of momentum from the larger body parts (muscle groups) such as the legs, hips and torso to the smaller body parts such as the shoulder, upper arm, forearm and finally the fist. This is also described as the distal to proximal sequence, distal being the most distant point from the fist (the feet) and proximal being the closest point to the

The Circus Punch

fist (the hand/knuckles).

Efficiency of punching is not the same as punching velocity. Efficiency measures how effective momentum is developed and transferred from segment to segment, the ultimate destination being the fist. Velocity not only depends upon efficiency of transfer, but also the magnitude of momentum created during this process. This is called the summation of velocities. That is, as the kinetic chain sequences from proximal to distal, each segment increases in velocity, as seen in figure 3.

Figure 3. The summation of speed principle (adapt)

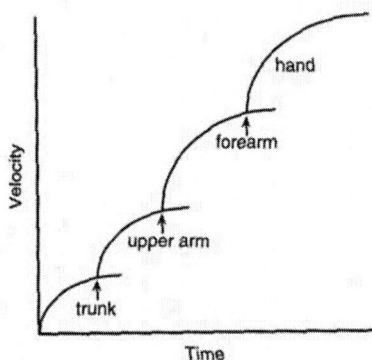

Figure 11.1 The summation of speed principle illustrated for a throwing example. Each successively distal segment begins accelerating when the contiguous, proximal one reaches its maximum.

Rotational Movement Equals Velocity

There are two mechanisms for transferring momentum along the kinetic chain. The first mechanism is inter-segmental transfer due to muscle activity. When a preceding segment in the chain has reached maximum velocity, the muscles connecting this segment to the next segment, such as hips to waist, contract at the point where the hips have reached maximum velocity. We have the velocity of the hips and additional velocity due to the pulling (contracting) action of the muscles between the hips and the waist, which transfers the momentum of the hips to the waist. This process continues up the chain as the sequence progresses to the arm.

The second mechanism, and one of the most critical in terms of fighters achieving maximum punching velocity, is the multiplier of the compound pendulum effect. The compound pendulum effect occurs when you have two or more masses connected in such a way as to rotate around a central axis such that momentum is transferred from one mass to the next.

A boxing punch has a specific set of body mechanics and principles, these 'rules' produce a sequential transfer of momentum from segment to segment. Increased velocity is the result of rotational motion, there needs to be an effect of lag between segments or otherwise if it is too rigid there will be no transfer (compound pendulum).

Punching involves a strength component and there is also a mechanical component. The mechanical component is how the body accelerates the arm using momentum transfer, the kinetic chain or kinetic sequence; the same principle that results in the cracking of a whip as the tip breaks the sound barrier.

The cracking of the whip when throwing a punch is the mechanical component and is totally dependent on body rotation. There are two primary sources of rotation.

1. Hip and shoulder rotation around the transverse body plane.
2. Rotation in the body's sagittal plane.

Figure 4. The body's three planes of movement.

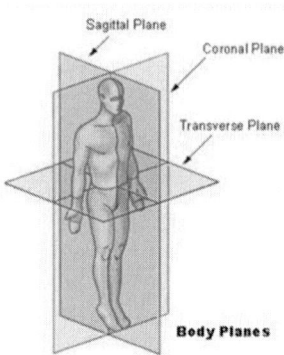

Coronal plane movement is side to side movement and is wasted movement with respect to throwing a punch. Imagine side to side rocking in the body during the motion.

Using the body to throw a punch – contraction to extension.

All movement involving the generation of speed and power must have eccentric-concentric muscle action. The eccentric is the lengthening of the muscle. Concentric is the shortening of the muscle.

Consider a two footed standing start to a long jump. A counter movement or squat first creates a longer distance to apply force and more importantly generates and stores energy in the connective tissue of the body. This counter movement prepares the muscles to reverse direction and provide more force in return.

For example, to achieve a maximum standing vertical jump height, a countermovement precedes the actual jump itself. The countermovement does several things. It creates a longer distance over which to apply force. The act of going down before reversing direction generates and stores energy in connective tissue, which then can be released in the opposite direction. And it more readily prepares the muscle to reverse direction and contract more powerfully.

This eccentric-concentric cycle is necessary in effective punching. The punch is loaded with body weight in the opposite direction then driving through the major joints of the body until it reaches the fist.

When the body throws the punch, all three planes come into play and interact, but which body movements result in the greatest effect on punching efficiency?

Basic punching instruction is usually focussed on rotation in the transverse plane more than any other body movement. Hip rotation is often used to describe or enforce what the body should or should not be doing when throwing the punch. The arm movement is discussed separately although the arm is the result of what the hips are doing.

The most efficient way to use the body to throw a punch is to maximize the contribution from both transverse and sagittal planes, this will optimally use both planes to create and develop momentum for the arm.

Ironically, in the fear of creating a punch with only arm action and not body involvement, the arm action in the punch has become one of the least understood components in the punch. For the punch to have power there must be an external rotation of the shoulder. Torso rotation (transverse and sagittal) creates the change in direction necessary to generate more force. Think again in terms of cracking a whip.

Another critical component is symmetry in the arms that produces force in the body. The nervous system of the body is initiated with an equal and opposite reaction. Jack Dempsey referred to this symmetry as the 'whirling shoulder'. observe this principle with the emphasis on retracting the non-punching arm. There is an appreciable amount of momentum that can be generated in the punching momentum plane as a result of the non-punching arm.

The final component is the completion of scapular action. During the punching process, if there is abduction of both the punching arm and non punching arm the scapular is contracted and extended which is optimal to increasing punching power.

The Soviets in their studies on sport science in the 1960s and 1970s understood these mechanics well. Their findings showed that 38.46% of the power of a punch comes from the legs, 37.42% from trunk rotation and only 24.12% from arm extension.

An American sport science study of Olympic boxers investigated the top major factors that contributed to punch power (wattage). The two biggest determiners of punch power were found to be:

1.   Hand speed (acceleration)

2.   One rep max (strength)
(The one rep max was measured in a cable movement to mimic punching action).

Somewhat of a surprise, both body weight (mass) and distance travelled (leverage) were shown to be far less important than the other two factors above. This again brings into question the assumption that a bigger person will always hit harder (force = mass x acceleration). One rep max is not correlated to the body weight of the individual, it is the ability of the central nervous system to recruit maximum muscle fibres for one explosive movement. Think of the brain sending a chemical message of nerve impulses to the body to fire it up. Leverage not being a major factor is equally interesting, bringing into question the assertion that a punch needs to be "wound up" and travel a long distance to be powerful.

Chapter Twentyfive: The Four Key Points In Punching Mechanics

The centre of gravity is the point in the body where the mass is evenly distributed upon which the force of gravity acts. When we punch, we need to transfer our body weight in the same direction as the punch. Jack Dempsey called this the 'power line' where all the movement of body parts are aligned in one direction with no 'leakage'. This is why a powerful punch is a crisp punch, with economy of motion and tight movements. There is no 'leakage'. An example is the uppercut where we add power by rising up on the hips and toes, sometimes this direction or powerline can be complimentary such as in straight punches where we sit down when we punch.

Understanding the centre of gravity helps us to be able to move both quicker and with more force. Dempsey called this the 'trigger step': to move forward he would lean into the front leg first, store energy there, then lift it and fall into it before bringing in the back leg rapidly. This results in both speed and transfer of weight; two essential ingredients for power. In punching we put that into action in three stages:

1. Move the centre of gravity.
    Once the weight is in motion, we use hips as a fulcrum to transfer the weight into the shoulders. The hips are normally where the centre of gravity sits, when they are rotated the whole body creates torque which amplifies power. Creating a hinge is achieved by placing your weight on one leg.

2. Add torque.
    Twisting the hips after transferring the weight is the equivalent of swinging a baseball bat out of the window of a moving car. This is an example of two complimentary directions to increase both speed and velocity.

3. Unload
    The final section involves releasing the kinetic energy into and through the opponent. To add force, make the movement shorter and tighter, like the so-called phantom punch that can't be seen. The tighter the arc of the punch with the arms close to the body the more torque and velocity will be added.

4. Changing the arc.
    In a modern boxing gym, you will most likely be taught the standard way of unloading a punch in a straight line with a quick retraction back on the same path to the guard. And there is nothing wrong with this, it's good basic practice. The fighters from the golden era were highly sophisticated in their punching mechanics and techniques. They knew things we do not today, things that have simply been lost and forgotten. One of which is the ability to change the arc on a punch and the significant additional damage it can

create. This really applies to straight punches, but by applying a slightly inward or downward reverse motion to a jab or cross it provides a hard torqueing impact. This acts like a slash and can both turn the opponents head and cause cuts. It takes some practice and feels odd at first, a classic example of this is Thomas Hearns's chopping cross. Persist and you can have something very special in your armoury.

Chapter Twentysix: The Perfect Punch

It is the short 8-inch punch delivered with a straight right. This is the perfect golden punch, simple, short and snappy but difficult to master. For this punch to be executed the mind must be 100% involved in the movement. It should be delivered with such speed and snap that the intention and signal from the brain must transcend the physical movement. In a street fight if this punch occurs it is often too quick for the eye and leads to confusion and bewilderment for an onlooker. In the boxing ring this is known as a phantom punch and comes with the same reaction of 'what just happened'.

It is a close-range punch that is set up by holding the left shoulder forward and the right hand is held back. As the left foot steps in the shoulders, waist and hips violently rotate as the punch fires into the opponent's jaw. It is an explosive action with all the movements occurring together in one split second.

This movement will need to be practiced thousands of times, it should never be a push but a sudden explosive crack, like bullet being fired out of a gun. The abdominals and diaphragm play an integral role and must be fully tensed at that moment, as if braced to receive a cannon ball.

Methods Of Execution:
- Light left straight followed by the short right, hit with the left quickly but without venom and momentarily hold the hand out for a fraction marking the spot before pulling it back and stepping in with the short right.

- Counter to a left punch – step in to the left and fire the short right. Even better against a left swing or hook as a straight line will always beat a curve.

- Set up with a left body hook, especially effective as the opponent is stepping in; immediately fire in the short right.

- As a counter to a straight left, step to the right and immediately twist and rotate the body fully into the short right.

- As the final punch in a combination of three it can have a devastating effect, first attack the body with a straight left, then a left to the head and then end it with the short right. Step in with the feet on every punch.

- Finally, this perfect punch can also be used to devasting effect as a body blow. Set up with a left lateral attack to the head, this should be a fast but not powerful punch, to distract and raise the opponent's hands. Immediately step in and follow up with the short right into either the solar plexus, ribs or heart. The elbow stays close to the body and the fist travels in a downward diagonal path.

Chapter Twentyseven: Mastering The Ability To Hit From Wherever The Hand Is

All good fighters can, in a split-second, hit from wherever their hands are. They can also deliver a knockout from a variety of different positions. The coordination of mind and body is a key principle in boxing and great fighters have sharp movements like an animal stalking its prey and a keen hitting instinct. This connection (trained or natural) gives the fighter the ability to deliver blows from any posture or angle, flat footed, on the toes, long range, short range, going in and going out.

To master this skill will give you the ability to be twice as good, twice as fast and twice as dangerous. There is a method of special training exercises with the heavy bag, a partner and solo that develop this skill by focusing on balance, leverage, footwork and rotation:

• Hit the bag from a long distance with straight left and right punches (jab/cross) move your distance in to very close until you are almost touching and keep hitting, then move back out until your arm is at full extension and keep hitting.

• Same as above except use lateral side attacking movements.

• Practice all offensive techniques instantly from a hands down position instead of guard or stance; jabs, crosses, hooks, uppercuts – everything.

• With a partner practice him rushing, coming forward while you move backwards, with straight punches.

• Practice on the bag moving in and out quickly with only right-hand straight attacks, the object is to develop quick knockout blows.

Chapter Twentyeight: How To Deliver A Knockout Blow

<u>Headhunting</u>
The knockout blow or 'sleeping tablet' generally occurs as a result of a sharp punch near but not actually on the point of the chin. This causes the opponent to temporarily lose consciousness and muscular control. It is a common misconception that the reason a lead front punch does not often result in a knockout is because it lacks power. The real reason is the exact point that gives the knockout is on the side of the jaw. So, the type of punch being delivered needs to have an element of lateral movement to it. Speed is the major factor at play, along with accuracy and penetration.

Essential components of a knockout blow include:

- Delivered with high speed and whipping action; heavy and slow blows will not be effective.

- Needs to travel slightly sideward unless the opponent's head is turned.

- The actual point of contact should be an inch to the side of the jaw, hitting on the actual chin will only drive the head backwards.

- Your opponent should ideally be coming toward you, never moving away.

An interesting component of the knockout is that it is more difficult to successfully execute as a standalone punch. It will have a greater chance of success in a combination of punches.
Footwork is essential to be able to generate force into the punch and should be clean and crisp. Likewise timing and delivery need to be spot on, with a coordination of the joints and muscles in the body.

<u>Body Snatching</u>
Attacking the body whilst not causing unconsciousness can end a fight with the opponent being unable to continue. The solar plexus and liver are the two primary targets to aim at to finish a fight by body snatching.

<u>The Art Of Punching</u>
Never:

- Hit with arm power only

- Develop slow heavy punches

- Fail to step in on every punch

- Tense the muscles or grip the hands

- Focus on lateral punches as your main arsenal

Always:

- Rotate the hips waist and shoulders

- Close the hand as the punch lands

- Extend the shoulders and elbows

- Step in with the punches (hands are connected to the feet)

- Ensure the hands and feet arrive at the same time

- Retract your hands at least as fast as they go out, never finish at a slower speed

- Concentrate on timing, meet your opponent coming in

- Focus on relaxation, tension is like applying brakes to your movement

- Separate a whipping punch from a heavy push, the later may put someone down but it will never knock them out

Chapter Twentynine: How To Avoid Being Knocked Out

In learning how to execute a knockout it is just as important to learn how to avoid one. Indeed, it is when launching an offensive attack that one is at his most vulnerable to a counter. It is the pay-off from having a more aggressive style. In the other way a very defensive elusive fighter is often not skilled at delivering a knockout.

Tucking the head and chin is the major defence and needs to be constantly practiced until it becomes a habit in all training. It is a formal requirement in boxing. Be particularly aware of it when you extend with the left hand and step in to close range.

Against a strong right-handed opponent, it is wise attack laterally with the left hand and circle away to your right. If punching with your right hand always keep the left high to protect the face and avoid the opponents right in a counter. Boxers in particular when they sense a right hand is coming will immediately try to beat their opponent to the punch.

Turning the shoulders in boxing and using footwork angles is also a good way to take the head out of the line of attack. At a very close range it is also wise to drop your chin to the chest to avoid an upper cut, we refer to this as burying the head in.

There are different guarding positions to protect the body and ribs, but they all share a common principle of defence – muscular contraction of the diaphragm and the abdominal muscles.

In boxing this is trained with specific abdominal and medicine ball exercises. Another good exercise is to practice sudden contractions of the belly, leaning forward slightly and shrinking your body as if reducing in height. 'Riding the punch' is another useful skill to master; the ability to move towards the punch when it is almost upon you, swerving your head and body, you will need to have impeccable timing and razor sharp reflexes to do this. It can be practiced in front of a full mirror to make the movements natural and instinctive. Speed is the key.

Practice shadow boxing moving quickly with attacks only coming from the left hand, attack 8 to 10 times at full speed all the time.
Stand side on to a punch bag left shoulder closest. Lean your body to your right into a deep crouch and extend your left arm to the bag and keep right fist cocked into the chin. Lean the weight back slightly. This position is technically a broken structure, but it is also a position that you can find yourself in when compromised. It is also a very deceptive and unorthodox position to launch attacks. It is very difficult for an opponent to hit your head in this position.

Practise hitting long range attacks from the above position, straight punches and lateral. With some practice you will find although a broken traditional structure you can still add significant weight and power to your punches by adding body sway and rotation.
In the above posture send out a straight left punch by straightening the right leg.

Practise the straight right to the body.

Still in crouch, fire out a straight left followed immediately by stepping the right foot in and an uppercut to the jaw

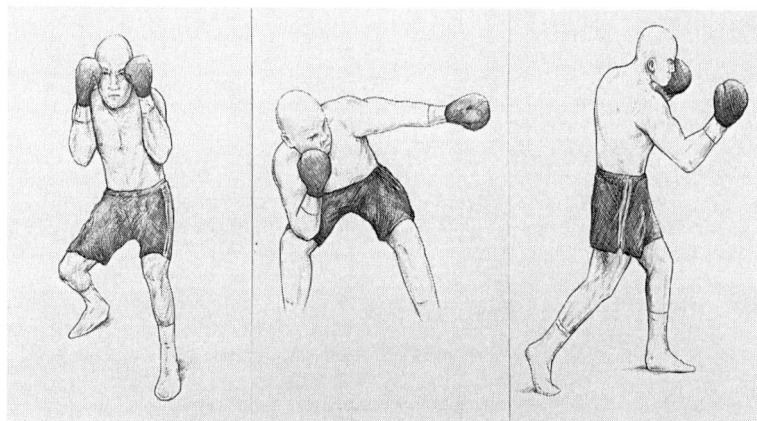

Chapter Thirty: When One Punch Can Change The Outcome Of A Fight

Even the most skillful and defensive boxers know the danger that knockout artist possesses. It is no coincidence that over the course of time the most avoided fighters have always been the great punchers that could wreck a career in a split second. People like Sam Langford and Marvin Hagler, who were either never given a shot at the title or made to wait and dodged like a bullet.

Julian Jackson was a man born with thunderous power in his fists, a devasting puncher who knocked out 27 of his first 29 opponents as a professional. In his lifetime he won the WBA Light Middleweight and WBC Middleweight crown on two occasions, he was more than just a great puncher, but this was his main asset.

Jackson ended his career with 55 wins 49 by KO and is listed at number 25 on the "100 Greatest Punchers of All Time" by THE RING magazine. The one man he wanted to fight was Sugar Ray Leonard who had promised the winner of Jackson vs Terry Norris a shot. Julian Jackson destroyed Norris in two rounds, Leonard changed his mind and chose to fight the loser, Norris. Some eighteen months later Jackson decided to step up from a light middleweight to fight Herol "Bomber" Graham for the vacant WBC belt.

Graham was a hugely talented boxer and chalk and cheese to Jackson, adopting a ridiculously wide side on stance and low guard. He would bend low at the waist, dodge and slip punches with incredible speed, reflexes and style. He was the defense genius to Jackson's antagonistic extreme punching power. A year earlier Graham had lost a split decision to a Mike McCallum for the WBA belt, losing points for low blows.

Herol Graham was hot favourite to win this clash and looked considerably larger than Jackson, who was stepping up. To make matters worse, the British Boxing board refused to sanction the fight due to retina damage found in the medical report for Jackson. It was agreed the fight would take place in Spain, and everything was looking to favour the bomber taking the prize. And that's exactly how the fight was going. Totally one sided in the favour of Graham, who was constantly beating Jackson to the punch, making him miss almost every punch and in total control. The superior boxing skills of the elusive southpaw Graham were shining through, even making Jackson look clumsy at times. Graham was more aggressive than his normal self, clearly set on a win. In the second round Jackson complained about being thumbed in the eye, the eye quickly swelled. Jackson was on the ropes taking a lot of damage from Graham who appeared to be getting even more confident as he dominated the fight.

In the third round, Graham danced and used his jab to sting Jackson whilst he circled the ring. A more desperate looking Jackson was off target and paying the price on every shot. With the eye looking progressively worse this fight looked to be stopped very soon. At the end of the round the ringside doctor told Jackson he only had one round left before this would be stopped. The fourth round began with Graham again going on the attack more. He could have stayed back and danced around more waiting for the referee to call it off, but he didn't, he surged forward. Big mistake. This fight needed a miracle if Jackson was to get out of this utter mess. Then it came. A thunderous right hand from Jackson came over the top of Grahams left and crashed down square into his chin. He was unconscious before he hit the canvass. In fact, he needed five full minutes to regain consciousness and spent the night in a Spanish hospital. The punch train-wrecked Herol Graham's dreams and he has subsequently been called the best British fighter never to win a world title. He had a 20-year career with 54 fights with 48 wins and 6 losses.

Jackson defended the title on four occasions and retired in 1998 with a record of 55-6 (49 KOs). He was inducted into the International Boxing Hall of Fame in 2019.

Herol Graham:
"The best puncher was Julian Jackson, come on, please. I don't even have to think when it comes to that question. One shot and I was gone and it came just after the referee was going to stop the fight in my favour. I made the mistake of going for a sucker punch, when he was in the corner, and Jackson responded with a knockout punch. I had to go to the hospital and there were some scary moments because I couldn't remember a thing about the fight. Three or four hours later it all came back to me and that was a really powerful right hand shot. There were a lot of broken hearts in Britain that night, especially mine."

Julian Jackson:
"Of all my knockouts that was one of the most historic," he said. "The fight was amazing. Herol was a very good fighter, fast as well; he was a big middleweight and he was"
"I got caught early in the fight, I think my right eye was swollen, the ref said if I don't do something, he's going to stop the fight. I switched (stances) so I could see him with my left eye and I literally threw the right hook since I switched to southpaw and he came straight in figuring he got me and I realized the punch was there, he was open. He came in for the kill and that's when I was able to get off my right hook and caught him flush on the chin."
In the above posture send out a straight left punch by straightening the right leg. Practise the straight right to the body.

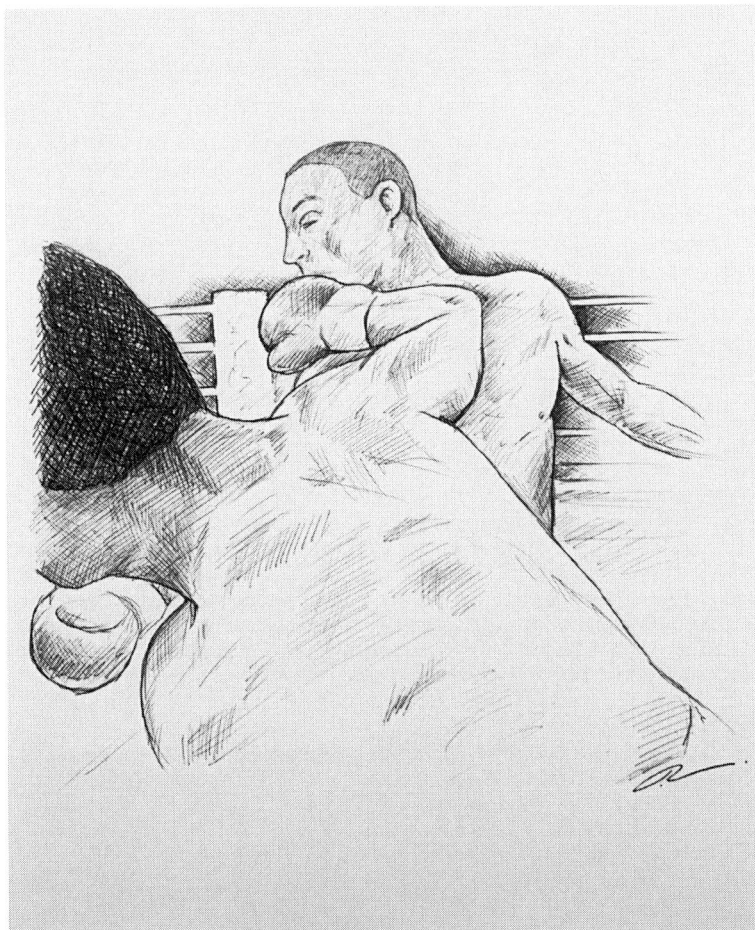

Julian Jackson

Chapter Thirtyone: Introduction To Old School Training

"Every boxer that has ever won a fight has done so by conscientious and faithful training"
Joe Louis

If we agree that old school boxers had a different way of fighting it make sense to acknowledge that training methods were different back then too. They were very different. Imagine the fictitious movie Rocky IV and the scene of Rocky Balboa training outdoors in the woods with limited low-tech equipment, chopping wood, lifting stones, and running. Then the Russian Ivan Drago in the lab driven by hi tech training machines and gadgets. Although filmed more than 30 years ago, the parallels of this movie very much apply today, indeed it was a homage at the time to the very old school, and that sweet science could defeat sport science.

Interestingly, in today's Heavyweight Championship we have two current fighters and champions that fall into each of these categories. Tyson Fury, the Gypsy King, very much from the old school from the direct line of generations of boxers from his father and even named after Iron Mike. He's been boxing since he could walk. Anthony 'AJ' Joshua, somewhat late to the sport, an intelligent young man groomed for success by Team GB, an Olympic gold medal winner with a six pack and muscles like a Greek god. Fury on the other hand is more reminiscent of a nightclub doorman, huge, uncut and with a closet full of personal demons he is trying to keep under wraps. Their styles couldn't be more contrasting. AJ is designed to demolish and destroy with bombs, not unlike Frank Bruno he has a very hard punch but somewhat limited head movement, fluidity, and classic boxing skill. Fury is a defensive master with a sixth sense of avoiding blows with very clever movement, he has also proved he can hit and destroy, just ask Deontay Wilder.

Joshua is trained by science and in the gym, he is an athlete who has adopted methods from CrossFit, bodybuilding, and sport specific programming to increase his muscle mass and strength. Fury embraces old, school conditioning methods, he even spent time at the infamous Kronk gym in Detroit with the late legendary trainer Emmanuel Steward, who has even cornered him in a fight.

So how did the champions in the golden period train back then? Firstly, they understood one thing; more muscles and raw strength does not necessarily equate to punching power; how many Mr Olympia or Mr Universe have been boxing champions? The old trainer understood that for the basic mechanics of punching to be effective there needs to be the following four components:

- Technique
- Speed
- Relaxation

- Elasticity

Any training programme must work to improve these components, not against them. Weightlifting (controversial) is not the best method for power in boxing. If you observe bodybuilders and people who lift a lot of weights, they also carry a lot of physical tension and tightness in their body. This in boxing is like applying the brakes mid punch. The body needs to be relaxed and expand like a piece of elastic to produce speed and velocity. This is applied through technique and joint alignment. The body needs to be connected as one piece to produce whole body power i.e. applying maximum weight into every punch (Jack Dempsey wrote the best description of this in "Championship Fighting"). Weightlifting and Bodybuilding is not modern or new, back in the days of old school boxers there were strongmen and physique champions just called different names, but their training methods would never be used in a boxing gym. So how did they train?

Firstly, it was holistic. An integrated approach to training advocating plenty of fresh air, eight to ten hours sleep per night, a balanced diet avoiding alcohol and taking regular salt baths. Everything was based on common-sense and tried and tested knowledge not fads. The great Bob Fitzsimmons said: "The great secret of proper training for all kinds of athletic feats is to use common sense. This is the keynote of success for all athletes. Common sense in eating, common sense in exercising, common sense in sleeping, all form a combination that brings one to success."

Old time boxers had a minimalistic approach of using nothing fancy or hi-tech, just proven, tried and tested, old school methods, which had been in place since the bare-knuckle days. This was based on:

- Sparring
- Roadwork
- Skipping
- Shadow Boxing
- Ball and bag punching
- Special exercises

Sparring was the main component, they boxed much more than fighters today. Of course, this was in addition to the high number of competitive bouts, which is without comparison to the pitiful number of fights professionals have today. Just compare the respective fight records, they speak for themselves. Sparring was also top of the list for training, old school trainers knew about specificity. Along with being the closest activity to an actual fight, sparring provides its own benefits to conditioning and toughening the body along with working the heart and lungs.

Any muscular strength work that was needed back in the day (with caution for fighters who needed to make weight) was achieved through calisthenics. Push ups, Sit ups, and Squats. Specialised neck and grip work. Exercises all designed to integrate and work the body as one piece, they lengthen and stretch the muscles, tendons and ligaments without tightening or disconnecting the body.

The power produced from such programmes is springy, light and fast rather than heavy, clumsy and slow. A missile compared to a cannonball though ironically one is a weapon from the past and one modern. In many boxing clubs today, we have gone the wrong way, seeking modern methods that promote a primitive result.

'I like to train. I always thought that fighting was mainly condition; to be able to go ten, fifteen rounds at a high speed requires good conditioning and that makes a big difference with a lot of fighters. Some fighters have ability, but they don't condition themselves properly. I always try to condition myself the right way. It's no effort for me. I enjoy it because I know it'll be helpful to me.'
Rocky Marciano

Chapter Thirtytwo: Sparring

"There is no substitute for sparring. You must spar regularly and often to become a well-rounded scrapper, regardless of what other exercises you may take. Sparring not only improves your skill, but it also conditions your body for fighting by forcing your muscles to become accustomed to the violent, broken movements that distinguish fighting from any other activity."
Jack Dempsey

No matter how much work you've put into the roadwork, skipping, calisthenics, shadow boxing and bag work, you will get very tired when you first learn to spar. This is why the old timers did so much sparring; nothing beats it. The more tension in the muscles the worse it will be, learn to control the adrenaline and be the master of it not the slave. Sparring also exercises muscles, joints and tendons in a way nothing else does, it is quite unique. Build up the number of rounds slowly.

Apart from being tired the other point you will immediately notice is connecting with your punches is much harder than it looks, especially when you are used to hitting the bag and shadow boxing. The speed, timing, balance, and positioning need to be spot on. What is the point in developing a knockout punch if you can't land it? When you first start out you will miss more punches than connect with them (which is also tiring) - your opponent will slip, duck, dodge and block them. You will also get countered and beaten to the punch. It's all a learning experience and with time and a good coach and sticking to the basic and fundamentals your improvement will be rapid.

"In boxing never have the muscles 'set' and tense. Always have all the muscles of the arms and body and legs loose and ready for action. Hold your hands open. Never close your fist, except at the moment when you land a blow. The reason for this is plain: holding your fist closed strains the muscles of the forearm and uses up a certain part of your strength unnecessarily. Always remember that you should never use any physical force until the moment arrives when you need it. Do not have your muscles strained and rigid. Keep everything loose."
Bob Fitzsimmons

No matter how sharp, crisp and fluid a man's movements seem, until tested in a realistic environment they are all theory without validation. Free form sparring is the best exercise one can practice to sharpen the tools, develop timing and distance and increase confidence in techniques. The ability to take, receive and recover from hits is equally as important as dishing them out.

Regular medium-contact sparring and occasional hard sparring is an essential exercise for boxing. Every training experience should be looking at improvement, learning and progression not sustaining injury or damage.

Controlled sparring, without being an exercise in compliance allows skill development in an environment with less adrenaline and panic where one can see movements more clearly and have time to work specific strategy. Being punished for making mistakes is not the most effective way to learn and develop skill, controlled sparring allows an environment to notice and work on mistakes that can be rectified then practiced at speed. It is also the perfect place to try new more complex movements.

Speed can be increased and then one learns the ability to switch on and off connection and power. This is an important ability, if you can only go 100% your skill is severely limited. By being able to go at 25/50/75 % power at will is a skill in itself that will lead to a higher level of full power.

In controlled sparring the body becomes more comfortable and able to relax, preserve energy, and integrate all the joints and muscles effectively.

Ground Rules To Establish:

- A hit is a light tap, there must be trust and confidence both fighters will not break this.

- Full relaxation should be present, this is no environment to get tense and excited.

- Constant movement should be present, it should be smooth but this is definitely a 'busy' exercise.

- No panic or stressed reactions, flinching, blinking, turning away etc.

- Range should vary, it is an excellent place to work on footwork.

- Don't be afraid to take hits to the body and face.

- Communication, discussion and analysis is absolutely encouraged.

No matter how fit you are it is all void if you don't put the work in with the gloves. Sparring is a learning experience, it should never be to intentionally damage or knock out your opponent, this is fighting; sparring and fighting are different. You will get hit but you shouldn't get beaten up. Mike Tyson famously said: "everyone has a plan until they get hit in the face". Make a plan and be well prepared for it. You have one job: to hit and not get hit. In every job you have good days and bad days so expect the bad days and get used to it. The first time it might cause panic, anger or other emotions; these need to be shut off. You cannot fight well under stress or red mist. Being a knockout artist is also about control, being in control and unleashing at the right time, when you choose to, not because your ego tells you to. Try to relax as much as possible, be cool, calm and collected

When at all possible, try to spar against opponents that are at least equal but ideally of a higher level to yourself; this will increase the learning experience. You must vary sparring partners otherwise you can get used to one style and know what to expect, the science of boxing covers every possible kind of style, you should box with tall men short men, long range, infighters, defensive and sluggers. You can only master boxing when you can hold your own style with any kind of style.

"Whatever your opponent wants to do, don't let him."
Sam Langford.

You need to learn to adjust your own style by playing to your strengths to exploit the opponent's weaknesses. The old boxing saying is: "Box with a slugger and slug with a Boxer". This means you can't perform if you play to their tune.

Sparring Tips Against Different Styles

The pure boxer:

• He likes to move around the ring and stay on the outside, always try to cut him off.

• Throw a high volume of punches, especially the jab to prevent him from using his.

• When he clinches, don't let him control the elbows and keep hitting with short punches.

• Use zig zag footwork to press him into the corners, don't just press forward.

• Body snatching will tire him and open the head.

The infighter:

• Keep away from the ropes and corners, stand ground and don't get backed up.

• If he gets inside, step to his outside and counter quickly.

• Use power jabs to keep him outside and off you.

- When he does get inside start to hit immediately, before he does.

- Control his elbows and shove him off you but be ready for the counter.

The slugger:

- He will try to come forward and land the big punch, keep moving and a tight guard.

- Keep using jabs and one-twos to destroy his balance

- When you see him plant his feet get out of range and move.

- Use counter punches and make him miss, this will tire him out.

The southpaw

- Everything is back to front so expect the reverse of what you are used to.

- Likely he will be power punching with the left.

- Infighting works well to close him down and prevent him using his strengths.

- Keep your lead foot on the outside of his lead foot by stepping to the left.

- Left hook and straight right combinations are effective.

"You can't be a star unless you spar, it's a whole different world inside those ropes, a world you can't appreciate until you've been in there, catching and throwing punches."
Joe Frazier

Chapter Thirtythree: Road Work

Though commonly referred to as running or jogging, in boxing its roadwork because boxers are out on the road doing their job. It's a massive part of mental and physical preparation. There has never been a successful boxer in the golden era who didn't do roadwork and very few in the modern. Roadwork is also a great way to lose excess body fat, it is very good for strengthening the legs and increasing the capacity of the heart and lungs. It should not be over-done, though in the past champion boxers have been known to run in excess of 10 miles per day, often in heavy boots for additional resistance and to further strengthen the legs. In the bare-knuckle days, they would run behind a cart-horse sometimes up to twenty miles.

The old boxers were smart and knew the concepts of specificity through interval training and would run the same length of time as they box, resting one minute between every three minutes. If you are out of shape start slowly and build up gradually, start at 15 minutes and slowly build up over 6-8 weeks to 30-45 minutes. the 10% rule of weekly increments is a good guideline to avoid overuse injuries. Joe Louis used to advocate squeezing small rubber balls in his hands as he ran to strengthen his fingers, wrists and forearms. Roadwork is also good for mental preparation before a fight, almost a moving meditation to gather thoughts and focus on the task in hand.

"No one wants to get up at 4 and run when it's pitch-dark, but it has to be done. The only reason I do it so early is because I believe the other guy isn't doing it and ...it gives me a little edge"
Mike Tyson

Chapter Thirtyfour: Skipping

An excellent training exercise to be done like your boxing schedule: three minutes to a round then one minute of rest. It is helpful in developing footwork and strengthening the ankles and legs and arms and shoulders, and of course overall coordination and 'lightness' on the feet. Instinctive moves of the feet are improved and perfected by the rhythm and sustained effort of the boxer who uses the rope. It has been said ten minutes of skipping is equivalent to thirty minutes of jogging. Skipping doesn't come automatically at first, you need to work on the skills of hand eye coordination and using new muscles in a different way.

To begin, throw the rope back over your head and rise on your toes. remember to be on your toes always. Bring the rope forward and as it passes before your eyes raise both feet lightly allowing the rope to pass under them. It is best to not skip with both feet first then move to alternate legs. Learn to bounce off one foot and then the other, which will feel awkward at first but come with time. Soon you will be doing double-unders, crossovers, high jumps and moving like an old school professional. With skipping you can either do rounds such as 3x3 minutes with a minute break or many of the old timers built up to doing 15 minutes straight with no breaks.

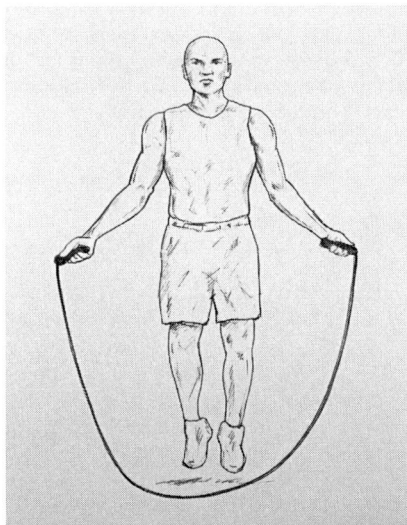

Chapter Thirtyfive: Shadow Boxing

Shadow boxing develops speed. Endurance and form. This practice has long been a staple of many champions, in fact in the olden times champion boxers were known to continuously shadow box for up to an hour nonstop! Can you imagine that today? They used to call it a 'memory trainer'. Now in modern sport science we class this as building the correct movement patterns and skills. The great thing about shadow boxing is it is creative, free of form and spontaneous, much like real fighting. Vary the style but be disciplined with the guard and keep the punches fast and snappy.

Practice as you mean to fight. Use your imagination to picture an opponent and use angles and slips to defend and attack and of course keep moving the feet. Practice at range, infighting, side steps, shifting. Repetition is the key. Imagine at the start of a round you face a boxer you have not met before. Feel him out, study his movements and make a plan. Use all the tools you have; this is the perfect exercise to both sharpen and perfect them. You can box multiple rounds of five or three minutes with a minute break in between. Ensure it is hard work and work up a sweat, don't fall into lazy habits.

Another very useful exercise from the past is dumbbell shadow boxing. Sport science may say this is not a useful exercise. The great champions would strongly disagree, and you can feel it for yourself. Use very light one- or two-pound dumbbells. This is not a strength exercise to develop the arms and shoulders but a speed and power exercise. Heavy weights will ruin and destroy punching form. With a light weight we can still retain the right technique and 'feel'. After a round of shadow boxing with the dumbbells, put them down and complete a round of shadow boxing without. Feel the speed difference and how fluid you feel. This exercise has been called useless in modern athletic training methods, clearly, they never tried it – it is gold.

Chapter Thirtysix: Heavy Bag

"Punching the bag is the best exercise for developing the shoulders, back and arms. It is the primary school of hard punching. Every muscle of every muscle of the body is brought into play. It trains the eye and schools the brain to act quickly. You gain in both delivery and defence"
Bob Fitzsimmons

The heavy bag has been used to great effect by all old school boxers. To get maximum benefit from the bag you need to be switched on and use your imagination and creativity to move around it, circle it, step side to side, slipping. Each time envisage the counter and imagine this to be a sparring session. The heavy bag plays a major part in conditioning and power development. It strengthens the fingers, hands, wrists, arms shoulders and legs. Your arms are just an extension of the body so use the whole body to torque and twist, like swinging a baseball bat. The bag is excellent as an expression of this coordination and synchronisation of the joints producing the power. Wear gloves and wraps to prevent injuries. Drill a minimum of 3 rounds of 3 minutes with one minute rest.

Some Tips To Get Started:

•   Commence with jabs and one-twos to the head. Move in and out keeping the guard high and the body and head moving and swaying. integrate hooks into the straight punches and suddenly move in close for a period of in-fighting.

•   Always have a plan when working the bag but not the same plan. Imagine a jab coming and slip left, step in with a right cross and place your head on the sack as you fire in short range punches.

•   Remember when close in not to use arm power, generate force from turning the shoulders and hips. Keep the punches snappy.

•   When finished infighting push the bag away with both hands, as you step back release a jab and short right hand.

•   Keep all punches sharp, explosive and snappy, don't try to swing the bag, try to fold it.

Specific Old Style Boxing Combinations:

•   Step in left jab to the body, immediately snap a left jab to the face, then reverse shoulders to fire out a straight right to the face. As the right hand goes out the right heel should be brought right up and push the ball of the foot into the floor. Ensure you get weight and reach into the punch.

- Fitzsimmons' shift. Step in with a quick one-two to the head. As the right goes in shift the feet, step in with the right foot as the hand goes out, immediately send out a hard left hand to the body.

- Dempsey Triple. Step in with a right body cross leaning to the left. Swing back sending a left hook to the body. Rise the body up and send through an over hand right. To ensure maximum weight into the punches the feet need to be shuffled in the following way: with the first right step in a little with the right foot. When the left hand goes in, step a little with the left. When the final right goes in, again step in with the right foot.

- Step in with a left jab to the face, immediately throw a straight right to the body. As the right goes forward bring the right foot up with it and loop the right hand over and up to the head.

- Four punches in rapid succession. Left jab to the body, leaning to the right. Right cross to the head. Reverse shoulders, left jab to the face. Lean to the left right cross to the body. Keep shuffling and moving your weight into the punches.

- Five punches. Two quick one-twos to the face, get maximum shoulder twist to ensure they are not arm punches. After the last right punch quickly send in a left hook to the body.

- Left jab to the body then a quick left jab to the face. Right cross to the body then a right hook to the jaw. Keep swaying g the body left to right and twisting and reversing the shoulders.

- Send in two quick left jabs followed immediately by a straight right to the face. Step in with the right foot as the right hand goes out. Finish up with a left hook to the body. Fitzsimmons, who made the shift famous, would often bring up the left from the body in a short uppercut to the jaw. Extend this combination to five punches.

- Leaning to the right send in three long left hooks to the face in quick succession, suddenly reverse shoulders and fire in a straight right to the body. Leaning to the right and slightly back on the hooks will ensure maximum twist and transfer of body weight into the punch.

Special Old Boxing Punching Exercise On The Bag

- Start with a jab to the body followed by a jab to the head. Then a double left hook. Follow this by a left jab and left hook. All the time keeping the right hand up in guard. Altogether three sets of two punches with the same left hand.

- Repeat on the right side three sets of double punches the same as above, keeping the left in guard all the time.

- Combine both the above into: left/right to the head, left to the body/right to the head, left to the head, right to the body.

- Three combination punches: left to the body, left to the head. Right cross. 2 jabs and a right to the jaw. 2 left hooks and a right cross. Left jab to the body, left hook, right cross.

- Ensure you can deliver 3 perfect punches within one second by saying the words "one thousand" in your head as you deliver them all.

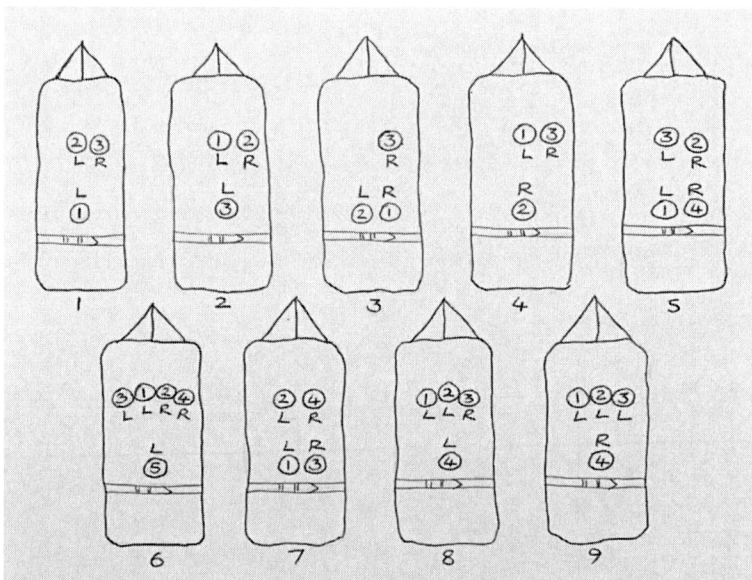

Chapter Thirtyseven: Top And Bottom Ball

A staple training tool in old gyms this device is sometimes called a floor to ceiling ball or a grasshopper. An inflated ball with two elastic cords fastening it to anchor points up and down. There is a reason why you don't see too many people use it these days, it's hard. Likely the first time you try to hit it the result will be the ball moves erratically and is impossible to control. Keep going. The benefits include substantial improvements in speed, accuracy and footwork all of which means power.

Do not hit all out because of the rebound, focus on smooth delivery. it will feel tricky at first, if you don't hit it straight it will wobble left to right. The harder you hit it, the faster it returns. It is difficult to build a rhythm but persist through clever footwork. This tool might just be the closest thing to a real opponent. Drill 3x3 minute rounds with 1-minute rest.

Useful Tips

- Lots of jabs and crosses and one twos. Long rallies for rhythm and timing

- Use footwork, step in and shift side to side. Meet the ball from different directions, practice delivering from and moving from different angles.

- Practice left hooks and right hooks at different distances, long and short and with pivots. Work the left hook off the jab.

- Left and right uppercuts. Many don't realise it can be used for this. You can by hitting beneath the bag where the connecting cord is. Fire in a right cross then meet the ball with the left uppercut.

- Fire a left jab, slip right and hit the ball with a right uppercut on its return.

- Set the ball going, catch it coming back with an open right hand, reverse shoulders and punch hard with the left. Next time meet it with an open left glove, reverse shoulders and punch hard with the right. Continuously vary the distance away from the ball.

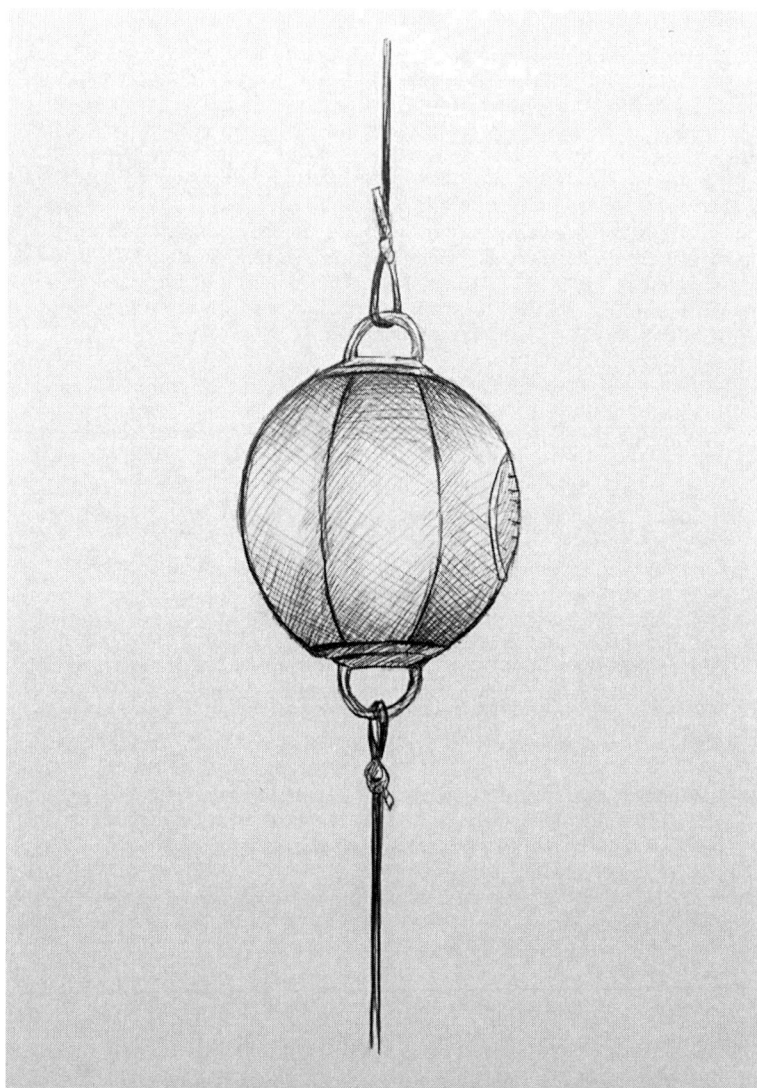

Chapter Thirtyeight: Special Exercises

Old school boxers mostly preferred to not lift weights at all, feeling it would not do them benefit in the long run. Although explanations given such as 'wrong type of muscles' and feeling they would slow you down, are generally not correct with the knowledge we know today from sport science. However, the main point to understand is that to be heavily muscled is definitely not a great thing in boxing. The supply of oxygen needed by those muscles over the course of multiple rounds is very taxing. Also, the positions of elbows and hands in boxing are extremely precise and being too well built in certain areas (particularly the chest) can be problematic. Another potential issue with weight training is the residual tension left in the muscles; this is why the old timers thought it slowed them down.

Boxing requires relaxation and fluidity and also a lot of sensitivity in the upper body when infighting. The old school boxers felt there were more efficient methods to service their goals. Likely they were right. Interestingly, this aversion to weight training continued into the modern era until the 1990's. A boxer who changed the path and thinking on this was Evander Holyfield. Holyfield, a cruiserweight champion, gained over thirty pounds of body weight through his body building programme, which was devised by a former Mr. Olympia called Lee Haney and the sports and conditioning coach Tim Hallmark. The success of Holyfield led the programme to be introduced to the US Olympic team and then of course the professional ranks. A big step in progress? Well, you can watch the video tapes of Louis, Liston, Marciano, Frazier and Foreman (who never lifted weights) and compare with modern heavyweights today like Joshua and Wilder who do lift wights. Certainly, they are much bigger and stronger than back in the day. How about the power, technique and boxing skill level; what differences do you see?

From a duration perspective the old-time boxers simply practiced more boxing in their training than the modern fighters. They were boxers first and athletes second. But that doesn't mean they didn't have other ways to train strength that they felt were more appropriate for their art.

Calisthenics

Calisthenics make you stronger using your own body weight as resistance. Physical and mental strength is needed in boxing. You don't need weights equipment and fancy machines. These exercises are old school but will condition your body and make you strong but importantly won't make you tense and tight like weights can.

Historically, routines were minimalistic, consisting of high repetitions of few exercises that they believed was suited to the grueling conditions of going twelve or more rounds in a boxing ring. These exercises were repeated hundreds and hundreds of times in multiple sets. Always at the end of training to not induce fatigue or tiredness for the most important part of training sparring.

Pushups

Multiple variations: wide, narrow, clapping etc. Some say the bench press is more effective; certainly, the bench press will make your chest bigger, but which exercises integrates your whole body, literally working every muscle together? It may be as old as the day, but the push up remains a great exercise.

Hindu Pushups

Sometimes called dive-bombers and having a tradition going back to Indian yoga and wrestling, these exercises are fantastic for strengthening and developing flexibility around the spine and hamstrings.

Squats

The legs drive power from the floor and transmit the force into the upper body through the hips. Boxers used to practice very deep knee bends to also increase flexibility and balance. This is also an extremely good exercise for the heart and lungs. Unlike push-ups which reach a limit before needing a rest between sets, it is possible to reach very high numbers of repetitions before taking a break.

Abdominal Exercises

It is extremely important that a boxer's abdominal muscles are capable of resisting hard blows and they have complete control of them. Daily practice of contracting and relaxing the abdominals was always practiced. You must have your stomach so well developed that your solar plexus and other vital points will be almost invulnerable to attack.

Practice the following exercises daily for as many repetitions as possible:

- Lying on your back raise your legs up to rest your weight on the shoulders, then pedal the legs as long as possible as if riding a bicycle

- Again, on the back raise both legs up high then make large circles with the feet together both anti clockwise and clockwise.

- The plough – lying on your back rock the legs back and forth over the head to touch the floor

- Full sit ups arms stretched behind head to touch the toes

- Windmills – standing legs wide apart touch each opposite foot whilst stretching the opposite arm to the ceiling.

Neck Exercises

It is critical to develop the neck muscles in order to withstand the impact of a punch to the chin. Here are three special neck exercises practiced by boxers in the olden times:

1. Using a small cushion on the floor take up a push up position with the forehead resting on the cushion. Press up to take the strain on the front of the neck as the body is raised in a 'V' shape. Take the hands away and repeat several times.

2. Reverse the previous movement looking up to the ceiling placing the back of the head on the cushion. Stretch up to a bridge without using the arms and repeat.

3. Place the palms of the hand on the forehead to provide dynamic resistance, work the head backwards and forwards twelve times, keep the resistance strong and get as much range of motion as possible. Change over the fingers so they are interlaced behind the head, work backwards and forwards twelve times. Finally work both sidewards motions using one hand on the side of the head and the other pressing the temple. Repeat twelve times each side.

Medicine Ball Work

The medicine ball has been around in boxing for a lot longer than people realise. The modern exercise methods from systems like CrossFit have adopted the medicine ball for explosive plyometric work, performing exercises such as wall slams. There is nothing wrong with this but the medicine ball had a multitude of uses back in the day, from extra resistance in calisthenics, body conditioning and even hitting. In days long gone by, trainers did not use pads or focus mitts, these came into use after the 1940's at the end of the golden age. Hitting the pads is great for accuracy, speed and fitness but the one major downside is you are constantly practicing by hitting someone's hands out of range. The range, angles and intent are not the same as in real boxing. The old school trainers understood the value of specificity and would hold the medicine ball at both chest and stomach level through multiple rounds while the boxer practiced body shots and head shots respectively. Not only is this more realistic but it also needs a great deal more power to drive through the ball on a person's body rather than a small pad on a hand.

Joe Louis, Rocky Marciano and Sandy Sadler and many other boxers into the modern area used the ball to condition the abdomen by having the trainer drop, throw and push the ball onto the front and sides of the abdominals. This tightens and strengthens the muscles and vastly improves the ability to take a punch. For example, you may practice this lying down in a sit up position and as the trainer drop the ball from a height you contract the muscles to absorb the hit. The same applies standing up as the trainer uses their body rotation to slam and push the ball into your side.

Other exercise with the medicine ball include:

- Sit ups – throwing and catching the ball going up and on return

- Leg raises – holding the ball with the feet as you raise and lower, hold the trainer's ankles behind your head.

- Alternate switching pushups, changing one hand on the ball in mid-air as you swap hands and complete a pushup.

- Squats holding the ball in front of the body for extra resistance.

"Those old timers were tough and in shape, the medicine ball helped them get there. You work the medicine ball right and you will be the tougher guy in the ring on fight night."
Joe Frazier

Wood Chopping
Several huge punchers have attributed one specific exercise to punching power including Foreman, Shavers and most of the old school – wood chopping. A fantastic whole body exercises involving focus and concentration and intent to hit through the wood. Most of the old-time boxers did this and a few still do today. It improves explosive power in the legs, back, shoulders and arms which are all the places where punching power comes from. Modern training has attempted to replicate this exercise to a degree with hitting a heavy sledgehammer on a giant tyre. It is not the same. For a start the axe is much lighter to also work on speed. Breaking the wood is a test of accuracy and focus as much as power. The same as punching.

"My real advice would be this: chop wood, lift hay bales; go back to old-school, natural methods of training. My trainer, Archie Moore, he told me to go away and chop trees for two weeks before a fight – and I did and it made all the difference in the world; all the difference to my life. I'd say doing things like that increases your punching power by at least 25 percent – forget lifting weights, that just makes you muscle-bound and takes away your speed. Weights are no good for you, that's what I say. Go back to nature when you train, that's what I did."
Earnie Shavers

Deep Breathing Exercises
Boxers in the past spent a great deal of time on specialist breathing exercises, this seems almost totally lost in modern boxing training, perhaps only retained in traditional martial arts and practices like yoga. They were performed to improve heart and lung functions which relate to both stamina and power in the fight. Here are basic instructions.
The following exercises should be practiced out in the open air ideally, or if not, in a well-ventilated room with the window open.

• Standing with your arms by the sides bring them straight up and over the body in a circular motion back to the original position. As they go up take in a deep powerful breath filling the lungs up completely, keep inhaling as the arms go up over and down. Using the leverage of the arms swinging back push the chest out as much as possible and pull the waist in and up. When you exhale drop the arms forward, round the back and cross the arms in front to one another. Then return to the side and complete again. Six to ten repetitions are necessary.

• Start with the hands together in front of the chest pressing together. Throw the arms backwards like a swimming breaststroke as you deeply inhale. Bring the shoulder blades together then lean forward, draw the waist in and up and exhale bringng the arms back in front of the chest.

About The Author

James Carss began a lifetime study of martial arts and boxing growing up as a teenager in the North East of England. A sport and Fitness graduate, James spent more than a decade living in Hong Kong studying martial arts fulltime and competing in boxing and martial arts competitions. He currently teaches from his home base in the UK and internationally, having students in Germany, Denmark, Italy, Slovenia, France and the United States. He is the author of 'Yiquan a fighting art' and 'Strength and conditioning for internal martial artists'.

Operation Sayers

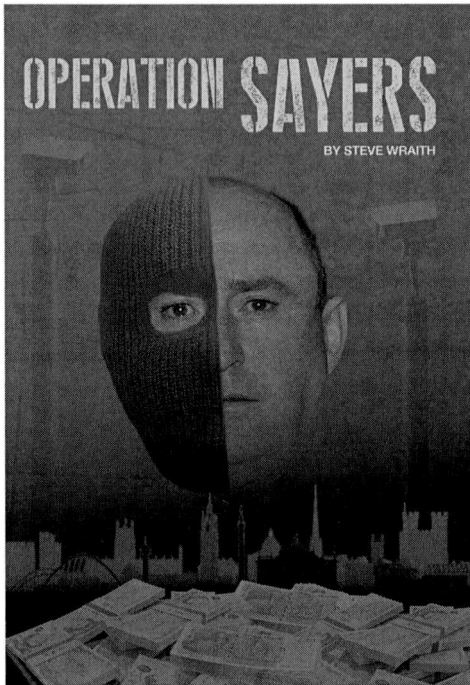

Operation Sayers takes a detailed look at the notorious Sayers brothers rise to the top of the criminal ladder on the backstreets of Newcastle's West End and the authorities attempts to bring them crashing back to earth by any means necessary.

The Sayers family were once described by 'Northumbria Police as a 'new breed of criminal.' Brought up in the West End of Newcastle by a career criminal father and a mother who was a paid up member of Mensa they were always going to rise to the top of the criminal tree.

The book exposes corruption at the highest level, the use of drug fuelled informants, and how one member of a rival family broke the criminal code to land Stephen Sayers in court. The book also reveals for the first time the full details of 'Operation Insight' which was set up to put Stephen Sayers in jail for the rest of his life.

Available now from www.badboysbooks.net

The Sayers: Tried and Tested At The Highest Level

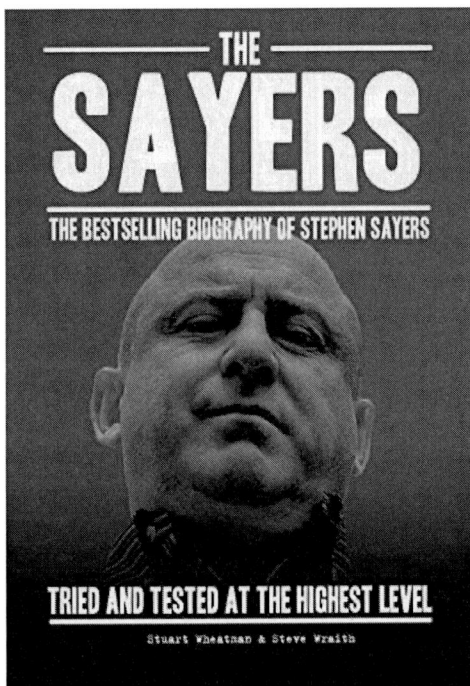

Stephen Sayers is one of the most feared men in the country, with a reputation that's preceded him in the dozens of prisons he's served time.

The Sayers family have been known on the streets of Tyneside for decades. No one else comes close to their level and it is widely known that they 'run Newcastle'. Rumoured to be behind countless violent multi-million pound armed robberies, unsolved gangland murders, extortion rackets and organised crime in general, Stephen, his brothers and associates are an unstoppable force. They've remained tight-lipped about their exploits... until now.

Stephen earned respect at an early age, blazing his own trail and coming out on top by any means necessary. A true bad lad in every sense, he gives us a first-hand account of growing up as a Sayers and living up to the reputation that the name holds.

Available now from www.badboysbooks.net